CAN ASIANS THINK?

CAN ASIANS THINK

KISHORE MAHBUBANI

UNDERSTANDING
THE DIVIDE BETWEEN
EAST AND WEST

STEERFORTH PRESS
SOUTH ROYALTON, VERMONT

The views expressed in this book are the personal views of Kishore Mahbubani and do not in any way represent the views of the Singapore government.

The author would like to thank the *National Interest, Foreign Affairs, Foreign Policy, Survival, Asiaweek* and *Peter Van Ness* for permission to reprint the articles in this volume.

"U.S. Doesn't Bear Excessive Share of U.N. Costs" reprinted with permission of *The Wall Street Journal* © 1986 Dow Jones & Company, Inc. All rights reserved.

Mahbubani, Kishore.
    Can Asians think? : understanding the divide between East and West / Kishore Mahbubani — 1st Steerforth ed.
        p.   cm.
    Originally published: Toronto : Key Porter Books, 2001.
    Includes bibliographical references and index.
    ISBN 1-58642-033-X (alk. paper)
    1. Asia — Civilization — 20th century. 2. East and West. 3. Values — Asia. I. Title.

DS35.2 .M35 2002
950.4—dc21   2001049723

PRINTED IN CANADA

FIRST STEERFORTH EDITION

In memory of my mother, Janki Mahbubani

CONTENTS

Preface   9
Introduction   12
Can Asians Think?   18
Asia's Lost Millennium   34

Asian Values
The West and the Rest   40
An Asian Perspective on Human Rights and Freedom of the Press   58
Pol Pot: The Paradox of Moral Correctness   80
The Dangers of Decadence: What the Rest Can Teach the West   92
The Rest of the West?   99

The Asia-Pacific
Japan Adrift   118
"The Pacific Impulse"   137
Seven Paradoxes on Asia-Pacific Security   158

Global Concerns
UN: Sunrise or Sunset Organization in the Twenty-first Century?   166
Bridging the Divide: The Singapore Experience   185
The Ten Commandments for Developing Countries in the Nineties   190

Notes   192

Index   195

PREFACE

On 11 September 2001 a new era was born. Unlike the Cold War era, which ended with a whimper, the new era was born with a loud bang heard all around the world. The terrorist acts of that day were outrageous and atrocious and rightly condemned globally. But they also tragically demonstrated that the era of isolation was over. All states, rich and poor, weak and powerful, now find themselves as common passengers on a shrinking globe.

Our world is shrinking in size, not in complexity. Societies and civilizations that had merely developed limited contacts with each other have moved inexorably toward interdependence; the lives of their citizens are increasingly affected by events and trends brewing across oceans that once seemed to provide vast and secure buffers. The need for cross-cultural understanding and sensitivity has never been greater, especially as new global coalitions are being created. This is one reason why this collection of essays, although written over the past decade, remain relevant to a North American audience. Their purpose is to open windows into the minds of the billions of people who live in Asia.

A year earlier, in August 2000, I was heartened to read a news report in the New York Times stating that Dr. Richard Nisbett, a professor of psychology at the University of Michigan, had discovered through laboratory studies that East Asians and Americans think differently. Dr. Nisbett observed that the Asians in the study "tended to be more 'holistic' showing greater attention to context, a tolerance for contradiction and less dependence on logic. Westerners were more 'analytic,' avoiding contradiction, focussing on objects removed from their context, and more reliant on logic."[1]

I have not seen Dr. Nisbett's study, and it may be too early to jump to any definite conclusions. But these findings do seem to confirm an intuition I have had from my life experience: Asians and Westerners do think differently on some issues. Mathematical truths cannot be varied in cultures; moral truths can. So too some values.

Looking back at my life after having completed half a century, I realize that I have had the good fortune of traveling through many different cultures and times. As a child, I was part of a Hindu Indian ("Sindhi") immigrant family in Singapore. My neighbors were Muslim Malay families. The society was predominantly Chinese. I was born a British subject, became a Malaysian citizen, and two years later, in 1965, assumed a Singaporean national identity. My education was always in English. Hence, all through my life I have traveled simultaneously through the East and the West. It is this life experience that informs the thoughts expressed in these essays.

The title chosen for this volume of essays — *Can Asians Think?* — is not accidental. It represents essentially two questions folded into one. The first, addressed to my fellow Asians, reads "Can you think? If you can, why have Asian societies lost a thousand years and slipped far behind the European societies that they were far ahead of at the turn of the last millennium?" This is the harsh question that the first two essays in this North American edition try to answer.

The second question, addressed primarily to my friends in the West, is "Can Asians think for themselves?" We live in an essentially unbalanced world. The flow of ideas, reflecting five hundred years of Western domination of the globe, remains a one-way street: from the West to the East. Most Westerners cannot see that they have arrogated to themselves the moral high ground from which they lecture the world. The rest of the world can see this.

Similarly, Western intellectuals are convinced that their minds and cultures are open, self-critical, and, in contrast to ossified Asian minds and cultures, have no "sacred cows." The most shocking discovery of my adult life was the realization that "sacred cows" also exist in the Western mind. During the period of Western triumphalism that followed the end of the Cold War, a huge bubble of moral pretentiousness enveloped the Western intellectual universe.

Even though some of the contents of these essays (especially the statistics) may appear a little dated, the arguments remain, I believe, valid. They provide one of the few antidotes to the sweet, syrupy sense of self-congratulation that flows through Western writing on contemporary issues. This is one key reason why this North American edition is appearing now. Several American professors have told me that these essays fill a void and provide a counterbalance to prevailing assumptions.

If my intuition is proven right, we will begin to see, for the first time in five hundred years, a two-way flow in the passage of ideas between the East and the West early this century. The world will be a much richer place when Western minds stop assuming that Western civilization represents the only universal civilization. The only way that the Western mind can break out of its mental box is to first *conceive* of the possibility that the Western mind may also be limited in its own way.

This book was originally published in my home country of Singapore. For this North American edition, I have added three new essays: "Asia's Lost Millennium," "The Rest of the West?" and "UN: Sunrise or Sunset Organization in the Twenty-first Century?" I have also deleted three essays: "The End of an Epoch," "An Asia-Pacific Consensus," and "The ASEAN 'Magic.'" In addition, I have written a brief introductory note for each of the older essays in an effort to relate them to recent developments. After some reflection, I decided not to revise these essays to update them. They have to retain their contextual consistency. It is the arguments, not the statistics, that have to stand the test of time.

Finally, I wish to emphasize that the views contained in this volume are my personal views. By no means should they be taken as a reflection of the Singapore government's views.

INTRODUCTION

CAN ASIANS THINK? Judging from the record of Asian societies over the past few centuries, the answer should be no — or, at best, not very well. Several centuries after Portugal burst out of its tiny seams to create colonies all around the world, from Brazil to Angola, from Mozambique to Goa, from Malacca to Macau, Asian societies continued in apparent stupor or stagnation, unaware that European civilizations — which had developed more or less on a par with Asian civilizations until the fifteenth century or so — had made a great leap forward. Societies that take centuries to wake up cannot be said to think very well. It would be foolish for any Asian to deny this painful historical fact.

By the end of the twentieth century, it appeared that a few other East Asian societies would follow Japan's lead and become as developed as contemporary Western societies. Then, in a painful repetition of Asian history, they lost their footing again. But having stumbled so often in their efforts to catch up with the West, Asians have an obligation to think — and think very deeply — about their prospects in the coming century and the new millennium. One key purpose of these essays is to stimulate Asian minds to address questions about their future. The lead essay, from which this volume takes its title, is intended for Asian minds. Its key message to Asians is simple: Do not think that you have arrived. The rapid economic advances enjoyed by some East Asian societies may, in retrospect, have been the easy part. Retooling the social, political, and philosophical structures of their societies will be a tougher challenge, and the moment to take up this challenge has arrived.

The other essays in this volume are intended for a larger audience. Almost immediately after the end of the Cold War, a mood of triumphalism took hold in Western capitals. Communism had failed, the West had won; mankind had realized "the end of history." Henceforth, all societies all around the globe, whatever their stage of social and economic development, would become replicas of the liberal democratic societies found in the West. The export of democracy from the West to the Rest was seen as inevitable and as an unmitigated good. However, as Robert Kaplan noted in the *Atlantic Monthly* (December 1997), the results of this global export of democracy have been less than ideal:

> The demise of the Soviet Union was no reason for us to pressure Rwanda and other countries to form political parties — though that is what our post–Cold War foreign policy has been largely about, even in parts of the world that the Cold War barely touched. The Eastern European countries liberated in 1989 already had, in varying degrees, the historical and social preconditions for both democracy and advanced industrial life: bourgeois traditions, exposure to the Western Enlightenment, high literacy rates, low birth rates, and so on. The post–Cold War effort to bring democracy to those countries has been reasonable. What is less reasonable is to put a gun to the head of the peoples of the developing world and say, in effect, "Behave as if you had experienced the Western Enlightenment to the degree that Poland and the Czech Republic did. Behave as if 95 percent of your population were literate. Behave as if you had no bloody ethnic or regional disputes."

By late 1997 (eight years after the end of the Cold War), when the self-congratulation arising from the triumph over the Soviet Union had died down, it became possible for some brave souls, such as Robert Kaplan and Fareed Zakaria,[1] to question the value and outcome of the immediate post–Cold War effort to export democracy. In the early 1990s, however, when some of these essays were written, there was no space in the Western intellectual firmament for anyone who asked fundamental questions about the export of democracy.

I can make this point with some conviction because of several personal encounters I had with Western intellectuals in that period, from Williamsburg to Brussels, from Harvard to Ditchley. In many of these encounters, I was put in the difficult position of being the sole dissenter to the conventional wisdom of Western liberalism at its moment of triumph. Several of my Asian friends confirmed that they had had similar experiences. The paradox here is that Western liberal orthodoxy claims that it celebrates dissenting voices. My personal experience suggests that such tolerance of dissent does not easily extend to challenges of the key intellectual assumptions of this liberal orthodoxy.

These personal encounters convinced me that there was a need to articulate an alternative point of view. My first printed response to post–Cold War Western hubris was published in the summer 1992 issue of *National Interest* in an essay titled "The West and the Rest" (and here I must record my indebtedness to the magazine's editor, Owen Harries, for suggesting this catchy title).

That essay was followed by "Go East, Young Man," published in the *Washington Quarterly* (spring 1994). It gained a notoriety equal to that of "The West and the Rest." "Go East, Young Man" was adapted from a paper titled "An Asian Perspective on Human Rights and Freedom of the Press," which I delivered at the Asia Society's "Asian and American Perspectives on Capitalism and Democracy" conference in January 1993.[2] This paper probably contains my sharpest critique of liberal orthodoxy. I have, therefore, decided to republish the full version here.

"Go East, Young Man" was followed by "Pol Pot: The Paradox of Moral Correctness" and "The Dangers of Decadence: What the Rest Can Teach the West," which was a response to the famous essay "The Clash of Civilizations?" by Samuel Huntington. It was my good fortune that Huntington decided to publish his essay in the summer of 1993. My responses to his essay seemed to travel almost as widely as his original. In the world of politics and philosophy, it helps to be read and noticed.

These essays that I published in the early 1990s, together with essays in a similar vein published by other Asians, helped to open a small new chapter in intellectual history. This chapter became part of what began to be called the "Asian values debate."

The term itself hints at a major misperception in Western minds of the message that Asian voices were putting across in the early 1990s. Many in the West assumed that any Asian thinker who challenged the prevailing Western ideas in contemporary social and political theory must be advocating the superiority of Asian values. Actually, the only point that most Asians were trying to make was that Asian values were not inferior. They were trying to say that there was a need for a level playing field in the new intellectual debate of the 1990s. With the advantage of historical hindsight, we can now look at those years and see that Asians were not marching out in that period to proselytize to the West. They were only reacting to Western proselytization.

One of the key flaws of the campaign to export Western values at the end of the Cold War was the assumption that the good intentions of the West in doing so would lead to good results. This is why, in my essay on Pol Pot, I quoted Max Weber: "It is *not* true that good can only follow from good and evil only from evil, but that often the opposite is true. Anyone who says this is, indeed, a political infant."[3] The moral complexity of transporting values from one society or civilization to another had been lost in the moral certitudes of Western intellectuals at the end of the Cold War. But this moral complexity was recognized by earlier generations of Western intellectuals. As Reinhold Niebuhr said:

> The same strength which has extended our power beyond a
> continent has also . . . brought us into a vast web of history in which
> other wills, running in oblique or contrasting directions to our
> own, inevitably hinder or contradict what we most fervently desire.
> We cannot simply have our way, not even when we believe our way
> to have the "happiness of mankind" as its promise.[4]

As we enter a new millennium, it is clear that the Asian values debate has subsided. Both sides have retreated from the debate with a sense of embarrassment, both feeling that they may have overstated their case. On the Asian side, after the spectacular stumble of several hitherto dynamic East Asian economies, there is a genuine regret at having spoken so confidently of the rise of Asia.

But these essays are not intended for any short-term ends. It is only a matter of time until Asian civilizations reach the same level of development as Western civilizations. The major new reality in East Asia is the genuine conviction and confidence among new Asian minds that their day is coming, even if they have to stumble once or twice more before they make it. Many Asian minds have now been exposed to the highest levels of Western culture, in the fields of science and technology, business and administration, arts and literature. Most have clearly thrived at these levels. The Asian mind, having been awakened, will not be put to sleep again in the near future. A new discourse will be initiated between East and West when Asian societies start to develop successfully again.

When this discourse begins, they will look back at the Asian values debate of the 1990s as only the first phase of a dialogue that will probably last for several centuries. At various points in the history of the past few centuries, when the West experienced its many ascendant moments — either during the peak of the colonial era or in the post–Cold War period — the idea arose that eventually all of mankind would be absorbed into the fabric of Western civilization. V.S. Naipaul, an Asian child of the West, captured this spirit forcefully when he spoke of Western civilization as being the only universal civilization. Indeed, for most of the past few centuries, any other prospect seemed inconceivable. The main historical legacy of the inappropriately named Asian values debate may have been to call attention to the possibility that contributions of other civilizations to the development and growth of mankind may yet equal those of the West. This is one key reason why this volume of essays is being printed. To ensure an accurate historical record, all the essays are reprinted in full. Thus, the reader will encounter repetitions of certain key arguments.

Having been born a British subject in Singapore and having saluted the British flag as a child, I had the good fortune to experience first-hand a clear historical demonstration that all nations have their ebb and flow. History never stops (or ends). In this shrinking globe of ours, as East and West come closer, many ancient civilizations will rub together in a direct fashion never seen before in human history.

It would be foolish to forecast the outcome of this close contact between civilizations. Huntington's vision of a clash of civilizations, frightening though it sounds, must be taken seriously. But again, as someone who has had the good fortune to experience the rise of the Asia-Pacific era, I remain absolutely convinced that the future lies in the fusion of civilizations. This is the vision I tried to present in a lecture I delivered at the International Institute of Strategic Studies (IISS) annual meeting in Vancouver in September 1994. *Survival,* the IISS journal, printed an edited version of this lecture in an article titled "The Pacific Impulse," which is republished here.

Over the course of the past few years, I have also published essays on various other topics. Some of these are republished in this volume. Given my conviction that the center of gravity of the world's economy will come to rest firmly in the Asia-Pacific region, I have written several essays on various aspects of the region. Hence, I am also reprinting "Japan Adrift" (written at Harvard) and "Seven Paradoxes on Asia-Pacific Security."

I published my first essay in *Foreign Affairs* fifteen years ago, on the Cambodian question. I am not republishing it here as that particular chapter of Cambodian history has closed. In the course of the decade-long debate on Cambodia, which became a modern metaphor for tragedy during Pol Pot's rule, I encountered another unusual strand in the Western mind: the desire to believe that there were black-and-white solutions to complex moral problems. It was in response to this that I wrote the essay "Pol Pot: The Paradox of Moral Correctness."

This volume would be incomplete if I did not include an essay on my own country. I am fortunate to be a citizen of one of the most successful developing countries of the world. Despite Singapore's success it has had the occasional misfortune of suffering bad press and has not received due recognition of its very special economic and social achievements. Hence, when the Davos Forum asked me to provide a short essay on Singapore's development, I was happy to do so.

Finally, in keeping with the spirit of many of these essays, I have decided to end on a provocative note by republishing "The Ten Commandments for Developing Countries in the Nineties." These ten commandments were written for a United Nations Development Programme (UNDP) conference on development, but they were reprinted and republished in English, French, and German. Brevity, I have learned, is universally appreciated. Hence, I will end my introduction here and let the essays tell the rest of the story.

CAN ASIANS THINK?

The Seventh International Conference on Thinking was held in Singapore in June 1997. The organizers wanted some Asian voices. When I was asked to speak, one question immediately popped into my mind: "Can Asians think as well as others?" The issue, I discovered, was a complex one. This lecture represents my first stab at answering the question. Its key aim was to launch a debate among Asian minds. This essay, an updated version of the lecture, was published in the National Interest *in the summer of 1998.*

My main disappointment with this essay is that it has not yet triggered a discussion among Asians on how and why their societies and civilization fell several centuries behind European civilizations. My own belief is that the time for this has not come yet. Most Asian societies (with the exception of Japan and the "Four Tigers") have not reached comfortable levels of development. When they do, this question will inevitably surface.

I am surprised, however, by the negative Western reactions to the title. Perhaps this is because the question is politically incorrect. But could it not also be a result of the fact that some in the West would prefer Asians not to ask fundamental questions about themselves or their future? For if they did so, it is conceivable that some might eventually become as successful as Western societies.

Any suggestion that some in the West would prefer Asian societies to remain backward would be dismissed as ludicrous by most Western intellectuals. But it would not be dismissed by Asian intellectuals. This East-West difference suggests that there is still a deep intellectual division in the world. One positive result of the 11 September 2001 events could be greater efforts by both sides to bridge the persistent East-West divide.

CAN ASIANS THINK? This is obviously a sensitive question. In this age of political correctness that we live in, just imagine the uproar that could be caused if I went to Europe or Africa and posed the question "Can Europeans think?" or "Can Africans think?" You have to be Asian to ask the question "Can Asians think?"

Given its sensitivity, let me explain both my reasons for posing the question and the context in which I do so. First, if you had to ask one single, key question that could determine the future of the globe, it might well be Can Asians think? In 1996 Asians already made up about 70 percent of the world population (3.5 billion out of a global population of more than 5 billion). By conservative projections, the Asian population will increase to 5.7 billion in 2050 out of a global population of 9.87 billion, while the populations of North America and Europe will remain relatively constant at 374 million and 721 million, respectively. This means that North America and Europe's share of world population will drop from 20 percent to about 11 percent. Clearly, in the past few centuries Europe and, more recently, North America have carried the larger share of the global burden in advancing human civilization. By 2050, when Europeans and North Americans make up one-tenth instead of one-fifth of the world's population, would it be fair for the remaining 90 percent of mankind to expect this 10 percent to continue to bear this burden? Realistically, can the rest of the world continue to rest on the shoulders of the West? If the Asian population doubles in the next fifty years, will Asians be able to carry their fair share of this burden?

Second, in asking this question I am not suggesting that individual Asians cannot think. Clearly Asians can master alphabets, add two plus two to make four, and play chess. However, throughout history there have been examples of societies that have produced brilliant individuals, yet collectively experienced a lot of grief and dislocation. The classic example of this is Jewish society, which has contributed more brilliant minds, in proportion to its numbers — from Einstein to Wittgenstein, from Disraeli to Kissinger — than any other society. Yet, as a society they have suffered greatly, especially in the past century or so. Let me stress that I am not speaking about the travails of Israel in modern times. I am speaking of the period from A.D. 135, when the

Jews were forced to leave Palestine, to 1948, when Israel was born. Will a similar fate befall Asian societies, or will they be able to think well and ensure a better future for themselves?

Third, the time scale in which I am posing this question is not days, weeks, months, years, or even decades. I am looking at the question on the time scale of centuries (this is especially appropriate since as I write we stand two years, away from the new millennium). Arguably, the future course of world history in the next few centuries, as I will explain later, will depend on how Asian societies think and perform.

In a multiple-choice examination format, there would be three possible answers to the question Can Asians think?: Yes, No, or Maybe. Before we decide which choice to tick, let me make a case for each answer.

No, They Cannot Think

I will start my discussion with the reasons for the No answer, if only to refute any critics who may suggest that the question itself is manifestly absurd. If one looks at the record of the past thousand years, one can make a very persuasive case that Asians, Asian societies that is, cannot think.

Let us look at where Asian societies were a thousand years ago, say in the year 997. Then, the Chinese and the Arabs (that is, Confucian and Islamic civilizations) led the way in science, technology, medicine, and astronomy. The Arabs adopted both the decimal system and the numbers 0 to 9 from India, and they learned how to make paper from the Chinese. The world's first university was founded just over a thousand years ago, in the year 971, in Cairo. By contrast, Europe was then still in what has been described as the "Dark Ages," which had begun when the Roman Empire collapsed in the fifth century. As Will Durant puts it in *The Age of Faith:*

> Western Europe in the sixth century was a chaos of conquest,
> disintegration, and rebarbarization. Much of the classic culture
> survived, for the most part silent and hidden in a few monasteries
> and families. But the physical and psychological foundations of
> social order had been so disturbed that centuries would be needed to

restore them. Love of letters, devotion to art, the unity and continuity of culture, the cross-fertilization of communicating minds, fell before the convulsions of war, the perils of transport, the economies of poverty, the rise of vernaculars, the disappearance of Latin from the East and of Greek from the West.[1]

Against this backdrop, it would have been sheer folly to predict at the time that in the second millennium Chinese, Indian, and Islamic civilizations would slip into the backwaters of history while Europe would rise to dominate the entire globe. But that, of course, is precisely what happened.

It did not come about suddenly. Until about the sixteenth century, the more advanced societies of Asia, while they had lost their primacy, were still on a par with those of Europe and there was no definite indication that Europe would leap far ahead. At that time, Europe's relative weaknesses were more apparent than its strengths. It was not the most fertile area of the world, nor was it particularly populous — important criteria by the measure of the day, when the soil was the source of most wealth, and human and animal muscle of most power. Europe exhibited no pronounced advantages in the fields of culture, mathematics, or technology (such as engineering and navigation). It was also a deeply fragmented continent, consisting of a hodgepodge of petty kingdoms, principalities, and city-states. Further, at the end of the fifteenth century, Europe was in the throes of a bloody conflict with the mighty Ottoman Empire, which was pushing its way, inexorably it seemed, toward the gates of Vienna. So perduring was this threat that German princes hundreds of kilometers from the front lines had got into the custom of sending tribute — *Turkenverehrung* — to the Sublime Porte in Istanbul.

Asian cultures, on the other hand, appeared to be thriving. China, for example, had a highly developed and vibrant culture. Its unified, hierarchic administration was run by well-educated Confucian bureaucrats who had given a coherence and sophistication to Chinese society that was unparalleled. China's technological prowess was also formidable. Printing by movable type had been in existence since the eleventh century. Paper money expedited the flow of commerce and growth of markets, and China's gargantuan iron industry, coupled with the invention of gunpowder, gave it immense military strength.

However, amazingly, it was Europe that leaped ahead. Something almost magical happened to European minds, and this was followed by wave after wave of advances, from the Renaissance to the Enlightenment, from the scientific revolution to the Industrial Revolution. While Asian societies degenerated into backwardness and ossification, European societies, propelled forward by new forms of economic organization, military-technical dynamism, political pluralism within the continent as a whole (if not within all individual countries), and the uneven beginnings of intellectual liberty, notably in Italy, Britain, and Holland, produced what would have been called at the time the "European miracle," had there been an observing, superior civilization to mark the event. Because that mix of critical ingredients did not exist in any of the Asian societies, they appeared to stand still while Europe advanced to the center of the world stage. Colonization began in the sixteenth century, and the Industrial Revolution in the nineteenth; both augmented and entrenched Europe's dominant position.

To me, coming from Singapore, with a population of three million, it is a source of great wonder that a small state such as Portugal, also with a population of a few million, could carve out territories such as Goa, Macau, and Malacca from larger and more ancient civilizations. But what is even more amazing is that it was done in the 1500s. The Portuguese colonizers were followed by the Spanish, the Dutch, the French, and then the British. Throughout this period, for three centuries or more, Asian societies lay prostrate and allowed themselves to be surpassed and colonized by far smaller societies.

The most painful thing that happened to Asia was not the physical but the mental colonization. Many Asians (including, I fear, many of my ancestors from South Asia) began to believe that Asians were inferior to the Europeans. Only this could explain how a few thousand British could control a few hundred million people in South Asia. If I am allowed to make a controversial point here, I would add that this mental colonization has not been completely eradicated, and many Asian societies are still struggling to break free.

It is truly astonishing that even today, as we stand on the eve of the twenty-first century, five hundred years after the arrival of the first Portuguese colonists in Asia, only one — I repeat, one — Asian society has reached, in a comprehensive sense, the level of development that prevails generally in Europe and North America today. The Japanese mind was the first to be awakened in Asia, beginning with the Meiji Restoration in the 1860s. Japan was considered developed, and more or less accepted as an equal, when it signed the Anglo-Japanese alliance in 1902.

If Asian minds can think, why is there today only one Asian society able to catch up with the West? I rest my case for the negative answer to our question. Those of you who want to tick No to the question Can Asians think? may proceed to do so.

Yes, They Can

Let me now try to draw out the arguments for the answer Yes to the question Can Asians think?

The first and most obvious argument is the incredible economic performance of East Asian societies in the past few decades. Japan's success has not yet been fully replicated in the rest of Asia, but it has set off ripples that now have the potential to become tidal waves. Japan's economic success was first followed by the emergence of the Four Tigers (South Korea, Taiwan, Hong Kong, and Singapore). But the success of these four tigers convinced other Southeast Asian countries, especially Indonesia, Malaysia, and Thailand, that they could do the same. Lately they have been followed by China, which now has the potential to overtake the United States and become the world's largest economy by 2020. What is amazing is the pace of economic development. Britain took 58 years (from 1780) to double its economic output. America took 47 years (from 1839) and Japan 33 years (from the 1880s). On the other hand, it took Indonesia 17 years, South Korea 11 years, and China 10 years to do the same. As a whole, the East Asian miracle economies grew more rapidly and more consistently than any other group of economies in the world from 1960 to 1990. They averaged 5.5 percent annual per capita real income growth, outperforming every economy in Latin America and Sub-Saharan Africa and even the Organization for Economic Cooperation and Development (OECD) economies, which averaged only 2.5 percent growth in that period.

You cannot get good grades in an examination by luck. It requires intelligence and hard work. Similarly, you cannot get good economic performance, especially on the scale seen in Asia, simply by luck. It reflects both intelligence and hard work. And it is vital to stress here that the pace and scale of the economic explosion seen in Asia is unprecedented in the history of man. The chief economist of the World Bank, Joseph Stiglitz, captured this reality well in his article in the *Asian Wall Street Journal:*

> The East Asian "miracle" was real. Its economic transformation of East Asia has been one of the most remarkable accomplishments in history. The dramatic surge in gross domestic product which it brought about is reflected in higher standards of living for hundreds of millions of Asians, including longer life expectancy, better health and education, and millions of others have rescued themselves from poverty, and now lead more hopeful lives. These achievements are real, and will be far more permanent than the present turmoil.[2]

The confidence of East Asians has been further boosted by the numerous studies that demonstrate the impressive academic performance of East Asians, both in leading Western universities and at home. Today many of the top students produced by American universities are of Asian origin. Educational excellence is an essential prerequisite for cultural confidence. To put it plainly, many Asians have realized that their minds are not inferior. Most Westerners cannot appreciate the change, because they can never directly feel the sense of inferiority many Asians experienced until recently.

The second reason why we might answer Yes to the question Can Asians think? is that a vital change is taking place in many Asian minds. For centuries, Asians believed that the only way to progress was through emulation of the West. Yukichi Fukuzawa, a leading Meiji reformer, epitomized this attitude when he said in the late nineteenth century that for Japan to progress, it had to learn from the West. Other leading modernizers in recent Asian history, from Sun Yat-sen to Jawaharlal Nehru, shared this fundamental attitude, but today Asians no longer believe that the only way to progress is through copying; they now know they can work out their own solutions.

This change in Asian minds took place slowly and imperceptibly. Until a few decades ago, Western societies beckoned as beacons on the hill. They were living models of the most successful form of human societies: economically prosperous, politically stable, socially just and harmonious, ethically clean, and, all in all, able to provide the best possible conditions for their citizens to grow and thrive as individuals. These societies were not perfect, but they were clearly superior, in all senses of the word, to any society outside. Until recently it would have been folly, and indeed inconceivable, for any Asian intellectual to suggest, "This may not be the path we want to take." Today this is what many Asians are thinking, privately if not publicly.

However, over all, there is no question that Western societies remain in many ways more successful than their East Asian counterparts: they uphold a standard of excellence that no other society comes close to matching, in their universities, their think tanks, and certainly in the realm of culture — no Asian orchestra rivals the performances of the leading Western orchestras, even though the musical world in the West has been enriched by many brilliant Asian musicians. But Asians are shocked by the scale and depth of the social and economic problems that have afflicted many Western societies. In North America, societies are troubled by the relative breakdown of the family as an institution, the plague of drug addiction and its attendant problems, including crime, the persistence of ghettos, and the perception that there has been a decline in ethical standards. U.S. government statistics tracking social trends for the period 1960–90 show that in those thirty years the rate of violent crime quadrupled, single-parent families almost tripled, and the number of U.S. state and federal prisoners tripled. Asians are also perplexed by the seeming addiction of

Europeans to their social safety nets despite the clear evidence that these nets now hold down their societies and have created a sense of gloom about long-term economic prospects. In previous decades, when East Asians visited North America and Western Europe, they envied the high standard of living and better quality of life in those societies. Today, though the high standard of living remains in the West, Asians no longer look on these societies as role models. They are beginning to believe that they can attempt something different.

A simple metaphor may explain what Western minds would see if they could peer into Asian minds. Until recently, most of those minds shared a general assumption that the developmental path of all societies was toward the plateau on which most Western societies now rest. Hence all societies, with minor variations, would end up creating liberal democratic societies, based on individual freedoms, as they moved up the socioeconomic ladder. Today Asians can still see the plateau of contentment that most Western societies rest on, but they can also see, beyond the plateau, alternative peaks to which they can take their societies. Instead of seeing the plateau as their natural destination, they now have a growing desire to bypass it (for they do not wish to be afflicted by the social and cultural ills that plague Western societies) and to climb higher in their search for a better life. This kind of mental horizon never existed in Asian minds until recently. It reveals the new confidence of Asians in themselves.

The third reason why we might answer Yes to the question Can Asians think? is that today is not the first time that Asian minds have begun to stir. As more and more Asians lift their lives up from the level of mere survival, they have the economic freedom to think, reflect, and rediscover their heritage. There is a growing consciousness that their societies, like those in the West, have a rich social, cultural, and philosophical legacy that they can call upon as they develop their own modern and advanced societies. The richness and depth of the Indian and Chinese civilizations, to name just two, have long been acknowledged by Western scholars. Indeed, for the past few centuries, it was Western scholarship and endeavor that preserved the fruits of Asian civilization, just as the Arabs preserved and passed on the Greek and Roman civilizations in the darkest days of Europe. For example, while Asian cultures deteriorated, museums and universities in the West preserved and cherished the best that Asian art and culture had produced. As Asians delve deeper into their heritage, they find their minds nourished by their own traditional culture. For the first time in centuries, an Asian renaissance is under way. Visitors to Asian cities — from Teheran to Calcutta, from Bombay to Shanghai, from Singapore to Hong Kong — now see both a newfound confidence about the future and a growing interest in traditional language and culture. As their economies grow and as they have more disposable income, Asians spend it increasingly on reviving traditional dance or theater. What we are witnessing today is only the bare beginning of a major cultural rediscovery. The pride that Asians are taking in their culture is clear and palpable.

In short, Asians who would quickly answer Yes to the question have more than ample justification for doing so. But I would advise them to pause first and reflect on the arguments for Maybe before arriving at a final judgment.

The Maybe Response

Despite the financial crisis in late 1997 and the travails that ensued, most Asians continue to be optimistic about their future. Such optimism is healthy. Yet it may be useful for Asians to learn a small lesson in history from the experience of Europeans exactly a century ago, when Europe was full of optimism. In his book *Out of Control*, Zbigniew Brzezinski describes how the world looked then.

> The twentieth century was born in hope. It dawned in a relatively benign setting. The principal powers of the world had enjoyed, broadly speaking, a relatively prolonged spell of peace. . . . The dominant mood in the major capitals as of January 1, 1900, was generally one of optimism. The structure of global power seemed stable. Existing empires appeared to be increasingly enlightened as well as secure.[3]

Despite this great hope, the twentieth century became, in Brzezinski's words,

> mankind's most bloody and hateful century, a century of
> hallucinating politics and of monstrous killings. Cruelty was
> institutionalized to an unprecedented degree, lethality was
> organized on a mass production basis. The contrast between the
> scientific potential for good and the political evil that was actually
> unleashed is shocking. Never before in history was killing so
> globally pervasive, never before did it consume so many lives,
> never before was human annihilation pursued with such
> concentration of sustained effort on behalf of such arrogantly
> irrational goals.[4]

One of the most important questions that an Asian has to ask himself today is this: How many Asian societies (other than Japan, which is an accepted member of the Western club) can be absolutely confident that they are on the road to as much success and prosperity as contemporary advanced societies in North America and Western Europe? If the answer is none, or only a few, then the case for the Maybe response becomes stronger.

There are still many great challenges that Asian societies have to overcome before they can reach the comprehensive level of achievement enjoyed by Western societies. The first challenge in the development of any society is economic. Until the middle of 1997, most East Asian societies believed that they were well on the way. They had mastered the basic rules of modern economics, liberalized their economies, encouraged foreign investment flows, and practiced thrifty fiscal policies. The high level of domestic savings gave them a comfortable economic buffer. After enjoying continuous economic growth rates of 7 percent or more per annum for decades, societies such as South Korea, Thailand, Indonesia, and Malaysia believed that they had discovered the magic elixir of economic development.

The events following the devaluation of the Thai baht on 2 July 1997 demonstrated that they had not. The remarkable thing about this financial crisis was that no economist anticipated its depth or scale. Economists and analysts are still divided on its fundamental causes. The crisis is still unfolding as this essay is being written. It is too early to offer definitive judgments on the fundamental causes, but a few suggestions are worth making.

On the economic front, many mistakes were made. In Thailand, for example, the decision to sustain fixed exchange rates between the baht and the dollar, despite the disparity in interest rates, allowed Thai businessmen to borrow cheaply in U.S. dollars and earn high interest rates in Thai baht. It also led to overinvestments in Thailand, in the property and share markets. All this was clearly unsustainable, and the International Monetary Fund (IMF) provided some discreet warnings, but the relatively weak coalition governments in Thailand at the time were unable to administer the bitter medicine required to remedy the situation, because some of it would have had to be swallowed by their financial backers. Domestically, a combination of economic and political factors precipitated and prolonged the financial crisis.

There was also a huge new factor that complicated the story: the force of globalization. The key lesson that all East Asian economic managers have learned from the 1997–98 crisis is that they are accountable not only to domestic actors but to the international financial markets and their key players. The East Asians should not have been surprised. It was a logical consequence of liberalization and integration with the global economy. Integration has brought both benefits (significant increases in standard of living) and costs (such as loss of autonomy in economic management). But there was a clear reluctance to acknowledge and accept the loss of autonomy. This was demonstrated by the state of denial that characterized the initial East Asian response to the crisis and clearly showed the psychological time lag in East Asian minds in facing up to the new realities.

Significantly, the two East Asian economies that have (after the initial bouts of denial) most fully accepted the bitter medicine administered by the IMF are the two societies in which the developing middle classes were quickest to integrate themselves into the new interconnected global universe of modern economics: South Korea and

Thailand. Although they continue to face serious economic challenges at the time of this writing, their elites are now well plugged in to the new financial networks. The new finance minister of Thailand, Tarrin Nimmanhaeminda, walks and talks with ease in any key financial capital. His performance is one indicator of the new globalized Asian mind that is emerging.

The 1997–98 financial crisis also demonstrated the wisdom in the Chinese understanding of the word "crisis": The Chinese word for crisis combines two Chinese characters representing danger and opportunity. Clearly East Asian societies have experienced many dangerous moments. But if they emerge from this crisis with restructured and reinvigorated economic and administrative systems of management, they may yet be among the first societies in the world to develop national immune systems strong enough to handle present and future challenges springing from globalization. So far, it is too early to tell — and this in turn reinforces the point that on the economic front, one should perhaps give a Maybe in answer to the question Can Asians think?

Second, on the political front, most Asian societies, including East Asian societies, have a long way to go before they can reach Western levels of political stability and harmony. There is little danger of a coup d'état or real civil war in most contemporary Western societies (with the possible exception, still, of Northern Ireland). Western societies have adopted political variations of the liberal-democratic model, even though the presidential systems of the United States and France differ significantly from the Westminster models of the United Kingdom, Canada, and Australia. These political forms are not perfect. They contain many features that inhibit social progress, from vested-interest lobby groups to pork-barrel politics. Indeed, it would be fair to say that political development in most Western societies has atrophied. But it has atrophied at comfortable levels. Most of their citizens live in domestic security, fear no oppression, and are content with their political framework. How many Asian societies enjoy such a benign state of affairs? Clearly, very few. And equally clearly, not many are going to attain it in the very near future. This, again, militates in favor of the Maybe.

Third, in the security realm, the one great advantage Western societies have over the rest of the world is that war among them seems to have become a thing of the past. The reasons for this are complex, but among those reasons are an awareness of ethnic affinity among Western tribes who feel outnumbered by the rest of the world's population and also a sense of belonging to a common civilization. The exhaustion of having fought too many wars in the past may also play a part. Nevertheless, it is remarkable, when we count the number of wars — and truly big wars — that the English, French, and Germans have fought with each other (including two in this century), that there is today almost a zero chance of war between the United Kingdom, France, and Germany. This is a remarkably civilized thing to have achieved, reflecting a considerable step forward for human history. When will India and Pakistan, or North and South Korea, achieve this same zero prospect of war? And if the answer is "Not in the near future," is it reasonable to suggest that perhaps Asian minds (or the minds of Asian societies) have not reached the same level as the West?

Fourth, Asians face serious challenges in the social realm. While it is true that it took the social dislocations caused by the Industrial Revolution to eradicate the feudal traces of European cultures (social freedom followed economic freedom), it is still unclear whether similar economic revolutions in East Asia will have the same liberating effects on Asian societies. Unfortunately, feudal traces, especially clannishness and nepotism, continue to hold Asian societies back, preventing them from becoming true meritocracies, where individual citizens are able to grow and thrive on the basis of their abilities, not their birth or connections or ethnic background.

Fifth and finally, and perhaps most fundamentally, the key question remains whether Asian minds will be able to develop a blend of values that will preserve some of the traditional Asian strengths (for example, attachment to the family as an institution, deference to societal interests, thrift, conservatism in social mores, respect for authority) and at the same time absorb the strengths of Western societies (emphasis on individual achievement, political and economic freedom, respect for the rule of law and for key national institutions). This will be a complex challenge.

One of the early (and perhaps inevitable) reactions by some Western commentators to the 1997–98 financial crisis was to suggest that it fundamentally reflected the failure of Asian values. If nothing else, this quick reaction suggested that the "Asian values debate" of the early 1990s had touched some sensitive nerves in the Western mind and soul. The desire to bury Asian values revealed the real pain that had been inflicted during that debate.

The true test of the viability and validity of values is not in theory but in practice. Those who try to draw a direct link of causality between adherence to Asian values and financial disaster have a tough empirical case to make, because East Asian societies reacted in various ways to the financial crisis. South Korea and Thailand, two of the three countries that were most deeply affected by the crisis (that is, those that had to turn to the IMF for assistance), had been given the highest marks by Western observers for their moves toward democratization. The three open economies that were least affected by the financial crisis were Taiwan, Hong Kong, and Singapore, which have very different political systems. In short, there was no clear correlation between political systems and financial vulnerability.

The only correlation that is clear so far is that between good governance and resilience in times of financial crisis. Good governance is not associated with any single political system or ideology but with the willingness and ability of governments to develop economic, social, and administrative systems that are resilient and able to handle the challenges of the new economic era we are now entering. China provides a good living example of this. Its leaders are not looking for a theoretically perfect political system. Rather, they search daily for pragmatic solutions to keep their society moving forward. The Chinese people support this pragmatism, for they too feel that it is time for China to catch up. Traditionally, they have looked for good government, not minimal government. They can recognize good governance when they experience it. The fact that Japan — which is in Western eyes the most liberal and democratic East Asian society — has had great difficulties adapting to the new economic environment demonstrates that political openness is not necessarily the key variable.

It is vital for Western minds to understand that efforts by Asians to rediscover Asian values are not only, or even primarily, a search for political values. Instead, they represent a complex set of motives and aspirations in Asian minds: a desire to renew the connection to their historical past that was ruptured both by colonial rule and by the subsequent domination of the globe by a Western *Weltanschauung*; an effort to find the right balance in bringing up their young so that they are open to the new technologically interconnected global universe and yet rooted in and conscious of the cultures of their ancestors; and a quest to define their own personal, social, and national identities in ways that enhance their sense of self-esteem, in a world where their immediate ancestors had subconsciously accepted that they were lesser beings in a Western universe. In short, the reassertion of Asian values in the 1990s represents a complex process of regeneration and rediscovery that is an inevitable aspect of the rebirth of societies.

Here again, it is far too early to tell whether Asian societies can successfully integrate themselves into the modern world and also reconnect with their past. Both are huge challenges. One clear advantage that Western minds have over Asian minds is their belief that their successful leap into modernity was the result of some special compatibility of their value systems with the modern universe. Indeed, many in the West believe (consciously or subconsciously) that without Western value systems no society can ever be truly modern.

Only time will tell whether Asian societies can enter the modern universe as Asian societies rather than Western replicas. Since it is far too early to pass judgment on whether they will succeed in this effort, it is perhaps fair to suggest that this too is an argument in favor of the Maybe answer to the question Can Asians think?

Conclusion

Clearly the twenty-first century and the next millennium will be very challenging for Asian societies. For most of the past five hundred years, they have been falling behind European societies in many different ways, and they have a strong desire to catch up. When they do so, the question Can Asians think? will truly be answered. Until then, Asians will do themselves a big favor by constantly reminding themselves why this question remains a valid one for them to pose to themselves. And only they can answer it. No one else can.

ASIA'S LOST MILLENNIUM

The millennium is a European event. It marks a significant turn in European, not Asian, calendars. At the last turn of the millennium, in the year 999, European societies were languishing in the Dark Ages, with little promise of shooting ahead. But shoot ahead they did, carrying human civilization to new heights of scientific and technological advancement as well as economic, social, and political development. If Europe had not shot ahead, most of mankind, including Asia, would still have been languishing in the feudal era. The millennium that has just ended should be called the European Millennium. And Europeans have every reason to celebrate this historic moment.

For Asians, this should be a moment of reflection. A thousand years ago, things looked more promising for Asian societies. China was enjoying the glories of the Song dynasty. One of the largest and busiest cities in the world was emerging in Southeast Asia, in Angkor Wat. Despite these promising environments, Asian societies slipped. They lost an entire millennium. Even now, only one Asian society — Japan — has caught up fully with Europe.

One of the key goals of my writings is to alert Asians that they have had no better historical moment than the current one to develop their true potential and, at the same time, prod them to be bolder in their ambitions and aspirations. If they get their act together, Asian societies could once again out-perform other societies.

But it will not be easy to walk out of a thousand years of stupor. Asians need to ask themselves hard questions. One of the key purposes of this essay is to look at some questions Asians should ask themselves at this turn of the millennium. How did they come to lose a millennium? Will they lose the next one too?

What challenges do they have to overcome to succeed in this new millennium? This essay, written for the special millennium edition of AsiaWeek, *attempts to spell out at least three key challenges that Asian societies face.*

"AT THIS HISTORIC MOMENT — when the ascendancy of Europe is so rapidly coming to an end, when Asia is swelling with resurrected life, and the theme of the twentieth century seems destined to be an all-embracing conflict between the East and the West ... the future faces into the Pacific, and understanding must follow it there."

Asian triumphalism, circa 1995? No! U.S. historian Will Durant, 1935. Asia has clearly been a land of promise. Yet it has lost most of the twentieth century — even much of the second millennium—while Europe and later America shot ahead in human achievements, colonized the globe, and took control of the world economy. The picture looked very different at the turn of the last millennium. China was reaching toward new heights under the Song dynasty. One of the busiest cities of the world was emerging in Southeast Asia, in Angkor Wat. Indian and Arabic societies were ahead of Europe in learning. And Asia's advance continued for several centuries. Then, for most of the past five hundred years, Asians stopped learning.

To avoid losing the next century, Asians must resume the learning process they have aborted for centuries. They have to ruthlessly analyze their past. They have to understand, for example, why so many Asians allowed themselves to be colonized by so few Europeans. What went wrong? They must further determine what went right in the West. Many would want to credit Europe's success to purely material factors: its domination of science and technology in the past five centuries. Superior European weapons subdued large Asian masses. But to look at the "hardware" alone, while ignoring the "software" advantages of European societies, would be a mistake. Distilling the wrong lessons may be even worse for Asia than distilling no lessons at all. And learning the right lessons is becoming more crucial as history fast-forwards into the next millennium. The velocity of change is accelerating. Societies with the right competitive advantages will leap ahead even faster. Those without will fall further behind.

Finding the right software should be easy. Successful societies exist. Best practices are visible. Why not copy? After all, Asia has copied and even improved hardware. But even the successful societies may not understand the real software fueling their success. The advice they give to developing societies, often with good intentions, has been simple: the key ingredients for success are democracy and free markets. Yet some societies, including major nations, that tried instant transformations to democracy have come to grief. So too those societies that tried free-market economics without the right institutional frameworks in place. Deeper principles explain the success of the developed societies. A short article such as this cannot provide all the answers. But let me suggest three key principles that may be found in the software of success.

The first principle is "meritocracy." When capitalism destroyed feudalism in Europe in the nineteenth century, it moved away from aristocracy toward meritocracy. Capitalism, with its essential ingredient of "creative destruction," generated new elites. Democracy provided another institutional process for flushing out old elites and churning out new ones. Both capitalism and democracy were therefore not purely ends in themselves (even though they are ideologically worshiped in many Western minds). They were also functional instruments that enabled — most times — new talent to emerge while simultaneously preventing the encrustation of old elites (which has been one key reason for Asia's failure). If each Asian society allows its best minds to emerge, flourish, and provide leadership, Asia could well take off. But conservative social and political forces resist change. And a great deal of Asian talent is wasted.

Globalization may succeed where domestic forces have failed. New economic forces are plowing through Asia, turning up talent. More than half of the 500,000 foreign students in the United States come from Asia. The American university system is the most meritocratic educational system anywhere. Asian successes there demonstrate that Asia has potentially the largest pool of talent to share with the world. Ostensibly this is a loss for Asia. Most will not return immediately. But many eventually do. Taiwan's economic miracle was helped by returning students. India's explosive growth in the computer software industry has also been helped by its returning "brain drain."

Multinational businesses — from banks and consulting firms to the dynamic new companies in information technology — are also tapping and training Asian talent. They could well be the yeast to revive long-moribund Asian societies.

The second principle is "peace." Peace, of course, was in short supply during much of Europe's growth. It took two debilitating world wars, where many of the best European minds were lost in mindless battles, for that continent to give up centuries of antagonism. One simple explanation for these two wars could be the time lag between changes in mental and physical environments. In the first half of the twentieth century, vestiges of a feudal mind-set — which saw war as a legitimate instrument for expanding power — persisted in Europe, even though the instruments of war had increased dramatically in their power of destruction. Nuclear weapons, paradoxically, may have finally removed this time lag.

Some Asian minds, including those of key policymakers, still linger in the feudal era. They see international relations as a zero-sum game. They have yet to learn the lesson Japan and Germany absorbed after World War II: power and prosperity can be acquired peacefully. The political dynamic of West Asia, South Asia, Southeast Asia, and Northeast Asia would become more comfortable if their leaders realized that peace is an essential condition for growth and prosperity in the modern world. Wars drive out investment dollars and kill (literally) talent. Peace does the opposite. Just one major war in Asia — between any two major Asian powers — could propel Asia back into the nineteenth century. Asians should learn from the wisdom of Deng Xiaoping when he said that future generations should be asked to solve today's territorial problems.

The third principle is "honesty." This sounds trite, but it is a polite way of drawing attention to one of Asia's most shameful aspects: corruption. Successful societies have functional elites. They add more value to their societies than they take from it. Unsuccessful societies have corrupt elites. As a result of feudal attitudes, they become easily entrenched, even though they survive as parasites. Corruption exists in both the democratic and nondemocratic societies of Asia (and indeed in other parts of the world). To successfully root it out, the rule of law has to be more firmly embedded in Asian societies. Corruption is a particularly pernicious problem because it is so difficult to document, except in the most egregious cases, such as that of Ferdinand Marcos. It thrives at all levels. And the costs are not purely economic. They are also social and spiritual. They breed cynicism and disenchantment, sustaining a vicious circle that has held Asian societies down: When there is no hope for change, why try?

And this points to the most dreadful truth that Asians have to come to terms with. Asian societies have not been held back due to colonialism. Nor have they been held back by inequitable international economic forces. The external causes are all peripheral (and often benign). The real reason that Asian societies have fallen behind European societies in the past five hundred years is a simple one: Asians have held Asia back.

But I do not want to end on a pessimistic note. There is hope for change. Globalization will generate new elites in Asia. So too will the increasing velocity of change. Huge numbers of Asians are being educated, at home and abroad. New global flows of information are opening the eyes of Asians. The "veil of ignorance" is being lifted. A new process of learning has begun. All these forces will generate new opportunities for Asian societies. But the first lesson that Asian societies must learn is how to develop, implement, and maintain the right software: meritocracy, peace, and honesty (MPH — perhaps a good acronym to remember in times of rapid change).

ASIAN VALUES

THE WEST AND THE REST

My year at Harvard, from September 1991 to June 1992, opened my eyes in many ways. One key insight I gained was that those who live and think in the West are not aware of how much impact they have on the rest of the world, or what the Rest thinks of the West. The Western mind believes that it understands all worlds, since it is open to all ideas and closed to none. The paradoxical result of this deep-seated assumption is that the Western mind is actually unaware of the limits of its understanding and comprehension. This essay, published in the National Interest *in the summer of 1992, was an attempt to open new windows in the Western mind.*

Of all the essays that I have published, two have gained the greatest notoriety. The first was this essay. The second was my response to Sam Huntington's "The Clash of Civilizations" (see "The Dangers of Decadence: What the Rest Can Teach the West" on pages 92–98).

Reading this essay eight years later, I am astonished how quickly some of my long-term predictions have materialized. In the essay I said: "In the eyes of the North African population, the Mediterranean, which once divided civilizations, has become a mere pond. What human being would not cross a pond if thereby he could improve his livelihood?"

When I wrote this, the illegal migration across the Mediterranean was a trickle. Now, in 2000, it is a river. European newspapers report these crossings with great alarm. But how could they not see it coming? The deaths of the nineteen Chinese hoping to be smuggled into England in mid-2000 in a shipping container provided more eloquent proof of the arguments presented in this essay than my words ever could.

Eight years later, the conclusions I drew remain valid. The image I used, of the defenders of Singapore in World War II with their guns pointing the wrong way, is still apt: there remains a strong impulse in the West to draw up the ramparts. But a huge contradiction is developing between the unilateralist impulses of Western political power and the interdependent and interconnected world spun by Western technology. When this huge contradiction explodes, I hope some will recall the points in this essay.

THE WEST WON THE COLD WAR, the conventional wisdom holds, not because of its military superiority but because of the strength of its social, economic, and political institutions. Hence, it is not surprising that a new consensus has quickly developed that the West merely has to hold a steady course in the post–Cold War era. Francis Fukuyama, with his celebration of the triumph of Western values, captured the spirit of the moment. The rest of the world, if it is to free itself from the "mire" of history, will have to adjust and accommodate to the ways of the West. Having already gotten things basically right, and facing no imminent threat, the West has no need to make major adjustments of its own.

This essay will challenge these widely held assumptions. It will argue that "steady as she goes" is not a viable option for the West; that while it may not face any immediate military threat, the West faces serious and growing dangers of other kinds; that it cannot afford to turn its back on the Third World because the Cold War is over; that in a shrinking and increasingly overcrowded world, in which the population of the West constitutes an ever smaller percentage, a comprehensive new strategy is needed; and that an aggressive effort to export Western values to the non-West does not constitute such a strategy, but will only serve to aggravate already serious problems.

Arriving at a sound strategy, a difficult enough task in the best of circumstances, will be harder because of the deeply ingrained habits acquired during the long years of the Cold War. There is a real danger that problems will be wrongly identified and defined, and that consequently the West's strategic sights will be pointed the wrong way. For someone of my background, this danger recalls the famous British guns of Singapore in December 1941. The cannons of that supposedly impregnable fortress were confidently pointed seaward as the Japanese came quietly overland on bicycles and on foot to conquer the island with embarrassing ease. This analogy is particularly apt because one of the most serious challenges that will confront the West in the new era will also arrive on bicycles and on foot, or their equivalent: the challenge posed by mass immigration from Third World countries. Superior Western military technology will be useless against these invading armies, because they will arrive as poor and defenseless individuals and families, moving without commanders or orders, and seeping slowly through porous borders.

If and when this happens, it will be only one dimension of a multiple crisis, a crisis resulting from the combination of a fundamentally changed Western attitude toward the Third World, and some well-known but inadequately understood secular trends.

The Retreat of the West

During the four decades of the Cold War, both sides attached great importance to the Third World. Seeing themselves as engaged in a global struggle for the highest stakes, neither felt able to treat any country, however small, poor or distant, as unimportant. Everything counted; nothing was irrelevant. Even as the West shed its colonial empires, the Third World successor states became more rather than less strategically relevant, especially for the United States. Because everyone else was already committed to one camp or the other, these countries constituted the main arena of competition, the contested hearts and minds and territories of the Cold War.

Although most Third World countries belonged at least nominally to the Non-Aligned Movement, that organization was incapable of providing them with effective security. For that, most felt they had only two effective choices: to identify to a greater or lesser degree with either the Western or the Soviet camp. Thus a ramifying system of patrons and clients, one with an elaborate if mostly tacit set of rules, spread over the globe. Third World states were by no means always the passive objects of superpower manipulation in these arrangements, and many became very skillful at exploiting the Cold War for their own ends. But it was a dangerous game, requiring precise calculation. Those playing it observed carefully what happened to countries such as

Cambodia and Ethiopia — two vivid symbols of twentieth-century tragedy — when they got things wrong. They also noticed that if the Soviets kept Mengistu in power in Ethiopia, the West kept Mobutu in Zaire. This was a time when strategic imperatives did not allow for exquisite moral scrupulousness.

With the end of the Cold War this state of affairs no longer pertains. Following the disappearance of the Soviet Union, Soviet proxies have either already fallen (like Mengistu) or been left exposed, without protection or subsidies, out on a very long limb. The West, too, has reordered its priorities. No longer is there the same compulsion to prop up unsavory allies in the name of national security. More stringent tests of human rights and democratic rectitude can be applied, and the inability of such allies to transform themselves at short notice to comply with these higher standards has been used as justification for abandoning some of them without feeling much in the way of guilt.

Whatever the ethical merits of thus using and then ditching allies, this sudden joint Soviet and Western abandonment of their erstwhile friends has sent a powerful message through most of the Third World. The rules of the game have changed; indeed, the game itself has changed. Third World regimes have begun to realize that their previous "usefulness" has ended and the West now sees little value in taking any real interest in their fate. The results of this are not all bad. The end of superpower competition has created the conditions for the ending of many conflicts that were kept well stoked by the Cold War, ranging from El Salvador to Namibia and Afghanistan to Cambodia. Many dictatorial regimes have disappeared. This is to be welcomed. But the removal of Cold War pressures also means that forces that have been bottled up in these societies can now erupt.

To understand the epochal significance of this new Western tendency to withdraw and leave most Third World societies alone (observe, for example, how many Western embassies are closing down in Africa; the British have in recent years closed their missions in Burundi, Congo, Gabon, Liberia, and Somalia), consider that these societies have been subjected to heavy Western involvement in their affairs since the colonial era started in the sixteenth century. The current Western tendency to disentangle itself from the Third World should therefore be seen as the end of an involvement that is not merely four decades, but four centuries old. All the indigenous processes that were smothered and subdued for centuries, either because of metropolitan pressures or because global forces were raging above them, can finally surface. To hold these historically pent-up forces in place, the Western world has left behind in the Third World a thin veneer of the Western concepts of national sovereignty, the nation-state, sometimes parliamentary institutions, and some principles of international law.

True, these forces were not totally bottled up during the Cold War. But since the end of that struggle they have been manifesting an acceleration and intensification that amount to a qualitative change. Tribal warfare in Africa, ethnic strife in Pakistan, Hindu-Muslim strife in India, Islamic fundamentalism in Algeria: all can surface freely now, with greater strength. The disintegration in 1991 of Somalia (one of the more ethnically homogeneous states in Africa) would not have been viewed with indifference — would not have been allowed to happen — ten years ago. During the Cold War the main political fault lines in South Asia were *between* India and Pakistan, fault lines accentuated by their superpower patrons. Today, the main fault lines are inside India and Pakistan.

The Shrinking Globe

In short, the reversal of centuries-old Western processes of intervention in the Third World is probably going to lead to the emergence of a cauldron of instability in most of the Third World. In previous centuries geographic distance would have insulated the West from this cauldron. Ironically, it was during the Cold War that Western technology shrank the world into a global village, destroying the insulation provided by distance and time.

Global communication networks that give the West a ringside seat when a Tiananmen explodes or a Gulf War breaks out have an equally spectacular reverse effect. Increasingly, once-remote villages in China, Central Asia, and the heart of Africa now have clear pictures of the comfortable and affluent lives of ordinary citizens in the West. Carl von Clausewitz observed that "once barriers — which in a sense consist only in man's ignorance of the possible — are torn down, they are not easily set up again." It is a remark worth bearing in mind in this context.

The simple practical effect of all this is that a single mental universe and a single global society are in the process of being created. All through the early and middle decades of the twentieth century Western societies had to struggle to remove from themselves the gross inequalities resulting from the early years of industrialization. This they essentially did. Now they are faced with a much, much larger proletariat on their doorsteps, drawn irresistibly by awareness of Western affluence and opportunity.

Western Europeans are beginning to understand this. If something goes wrong in, say, Algeria or Tunisia, the problems will have an effect on France. In the eyes of the North African population, the Mediterranean, which once divided civilizations, has become a mere pond. What human being would not cross a pond if thereby he could improve his livelihood? Through all previous centuries men and women have crossed oceans and mountains to seek a better life, often suffering terrible hardship in the process. Indeed, it is this drive that explains the wide geographic span of "Western" societies outside their origins in continental Europe, stretching from North America to South Africa, to Australia and New Zealand. Today, many more people feel that they can make similar journeys. So far, Western Europeans have only seen the beginnings of such mass movements, and already they are deeply troubled.

In 1990 the ratio of Europe's population to that of Africa was 498 million to 642 million; according to UN projections, by 2050, based on medium fertility extension, the ratio will be 486 million (a decrease, be it noted) to 2.265 billion — that is, a ratio akin to the white-black ratio in today's South Africa. Two nations, currently of the same population size, demonstrate the meaning of this trend. In the past few years, despite net immigration, Italy's population has been declining. Egypt's is growing by a million every eight months. Italy reacted very harshly to the Albanian boat people. How much more harshly would it react if the boat people were not fellow Europeans? Or consider this: In 1960 the combined population of Morocco and Algeria amounted to half that of France; today it is about equal; in another thirty years it will be double that of France.

To put it simply, within a few decades, when Western Europe is confronted with teeming impoverished masses on its borders and when increasing numbers are daily slipping in to join the millions already there, Europeans will find themselves in essentially the same strategic plight as the affluent but vastly outnumbered white population of South Africa today.

Even the United States, separated from the fast-growing population centers of Asia and Africa by two mighty oceans, is not immune. As Ivan Head observes, "North America is home to one of the fastest growing of all national populations. The population of Mexico in 1950 was 25 million. Before this decade concludes, it will be 100 million." Despite the magnetic power of U.S. popular culture (which once made even the French feel threatened), some of the southwestern states of the United States are effectively becoming bilingual societies, reflecting the great influx from the south. At what point will the nature of U.S. society and culture change irreversibly?

The term "population explosion" is disarmingly familiar, a cliché. But like many clichés it expresses a vital truth. From 1750 to 1950 the populations of the five main continents grew at about the same rate. After 1950 there was a dramatic surge of population growth in the Third World, largely resulting from the spread of Western methods of hygiene and basic health care. The population balance between Europe and North America and the rest of the world has been irretrievably altered. In the year 2000 (a mere eight years away), out of a projected global population of 6.25 billion, 5 billion will live in the Third World. Ninety-seven percent of the world's population increase will take place in the Third World.

Population numbers matter. When there are extreme differences, they create the sort of security dilemmas that, in their different ways, nations such as Israel, Mongolia, Nepal, and white South Africa face. Even in the absence of such conventional security threats, this population imbalance, aggravated by the enormous disparity in living standards, will be the fundamental underlying cause of new threats to the stability of the Western world, ranging from migrations of the poor and dispossessed to environmental damage, drugs, disease, and terrorism.

The Impact of East Asia

The stark picture of an affluent West and a poor Third World is complicated and confused by the increasing importance of the East Asians, the only non-Westerners already in, or poised to enter, the world of developed nations. Though their economic success, especially that of Japan, is seen as a serious problem by some in the West, in the larger context of relations between the West and the Rest it surely should be seen as part of the solution. For Japan and the other East Asian success stories are setting off ripples of development in the Third World in a way that no Western society has ever succeeded in doing.

Consider this great historical oddity: Why is it that decades of proximity to, and contact with, North America and Western Europe did not inspire any of the neighboring societies in Latin America, the Middle East, or Africa to plunge into the free-market universe, despite the obvious economic benefits of doing so? Why is Japan the only developed nation to stimulate such emulation?

The answer will inevitably be complex, but one critical factor, largely overlooked, has been the psychological. In 1905, when Japan, an Asian nation, defeated Russia, a white power, it unintentionally provided a tremendous psychological boost to anticolonialism. If not the vast majority, then at least the emerging educated elites of non-European countries could, for the first time, conceive of the possibility that colonial subjugation was not necessarily a permanent condition, a state of nature. The generation of Jawaharlal Nehru, a boy of fourteen at the time of the war, was greatly stirred.

Today, Japan's economic success is having a similar psychological impact on developing societies all over the world, gradually convincing them that they too can make it into the developed universe. This psychological leap is crucial. Until recently, most Third World nations believed subconsciously that developed status was out of their reach. Today, after looking at Japan and its neighbors, many believe otherwise.

Japan did not intend this. Global benevolence has not yet infused the character of the Japanese. But its success convinced its neighbors, ranging from Korea to Taiwan to Singapore, that they too could do it. Their success has, in turn, had a significant effect on China. The economic takeoff of China's coastal provinces has reduced the ability of Beijing to reverse course from economic liberalization and has also helped convince Indonesia, the world's fifth most populous nation, to deregulate even faster, suggesting that a new economic synergy is developing in East Asia.

But the effect is not restricted to the region. Largely unnoticed, pilgrims from all other parts of the world have been coming to East Asia to observe and learn. Turks and Mexicans, Iranians and Chileans are fascinated by East Asia's success. If the East Asians can do it, why can't they? So far, no Islamic nation has successfully modernized. But if Malaysia and Indonesia, two Muslim countries far from the birthplace of Islam, can be swept upward by the rising Asia-Pacific economic tide — and the process is well under way — the winds in the Islamic world will no longer move from West to East Asia but in the reverse direction, a major historic change. Over time, countries such as Algeria and Tunisia may also be drawn into this process.

Looked at in this way, Europe and North America, which are increasingly feeling threatened by Japan's economic advance, may indeed have a vested interest in its progress. If the belief and expectation of economic development can be planted in the minds of billions of people, massive migrations may be averted. Those Western Europeans who are already fearful of such migrations from North Africa should do some fundamental strategic rethinking and begin viewing the challenge from East Asia in a different light. What in the short term presents a problem could bring long-term strategic redemption.

Economic Horses, Democratic Carts

As the numbers mount and the prospect of ever worsening poverty and mass migration looms, most of those Westerners who have not become entirely indifferent to the Third World seem to be determined that first priority must be given to the promotion of human rights and democracy. For the first time since decolonization, many countries have been told that development aid, even from multilateral institutions such as the UN Development Program, will be conditional upon moves toward democratization. This campaign for democracy and human rights in the Third World could backfire badly and undermine Western security in the post–Cold War era.

The collapse of Communism in the face of challenges from democracies has given a powerful new burst of confidence to believers in democratic values. These values strengthen the social and political fabric of Western societies, because they involve all citizens in national affairs and hence develop in the citizens a commitment to their society. In addition, democratic systems lead to constant circulation within the ruling elites, thereby ensuring the infusion of new blood and new ideas into critical councils. As well as the moral strength of these values, their functional strengths will enhance the global trend toward democratization and increasing respect for human rights. Those that fail to adapt to this trend are likely to suffer in the long-term Darwinian contest between societies. Japan, for example, could remain far ahead of China for centuries if China fails to create a system that will enable it to extract and use its human talent as effectively as Japan.

The question remains, however: How does one successfully transplant democracy into societies that historically have had very different social and political systems? The assumption in some American political and intellectual circles today seems to be that any society, including China, can make this transition virtually immediately. Yet most Western societies (including the most recent cases, such as Spain and Portugal) did not make the leap overnight from traditional or semifeudal systems. Economic development came first, creating both working and middle classes that had a vested interest in stability and would therefore not be pulled apart by demagogic democratic politicians trying to capitalize on ethnic and other sectional differences. That has also been the path taken by those who have made the successful transition to democracy in East Asia.

Today the West is encouraging, and sometimes demanding, the opposite approach in the Third World. It is promoting democracy *before* economic development. It assumes that democracy can be successfully transplanted into societies that are at low levels of economic development and that are deeply divided socially across many lines — tribal, ethnic, and religious, among others. In a developed and industrialized society a democratic system draws in the established middle class that has a vested interest in stability. In many Asian and African cases, without such middle classes, the national polity breaks down into ethnic and tribal loyalties. If this in turn leads to internecine warfare, can one argue that democracy will always bring beneficial consequences?

As far back as 1861, John Stuart Mill said that democracy is "next to impossible in a country made up of different nationalities." Even earlier, John Jay, writing in the *Federalist*, stressed that Americans were "descended from the same ancestors, speaking the same language, professing the same religion, attached to the same principles of government, very similar in their manners and customs." He added that they were surely "a band of brethren" and "should never be split into a number of unsocial, jealous and alien sovereignties." Earlier theorists of democracy would be surprised by the twentieth-century conceit that democracy can be applied to any society, regardless of its stage of development or its internal social divisions.

To avoid misunderstanding, let me stress that I am not arguing that democratic systems are necessarily antithetical to development in contemporary Third World societies. Theoretically, it is possible to have both. In some cases, it may even work. But a calm and dispassionate look at Third World conditions suggests that a period of government that is strong, firm, and committed to radical reform may be necessary to break out of the vicious circle of poverty sustained by social structures that contain vested interests opposed to any real changes. Japan was able to go into high growth after World War II in part because of the wide-ranging socioeconomic reforms that General MacArthur imposed. No democratically elected Japanese government could have done what he did. By contrast, the failure of the United States to carry out similar socioeconomic reforms in the Philippines is one reason why the economy of that country has not developed well in the postwar years.

Of course, the Filipino case demonstrates that authoritarian governments can be antithetical to development. However, it is equally true that some authoritarian governments have been good for development, as is shown by the dramatic economic growth of South Korea and Taiwan in the early years. The point here is simple: the crucial variable in determining whether a Third World society will progress is not whether its government is democratic but whether, to put it simply, it has "good government."

"Good government" is hard to define, especially in the American context, where the term is almost an oxymoron. In the United States good government often means the least government. In Third World societies, burdened with huge development demands, the common characteristics found in the successful East Asian societies may help to provide a useful definition of "good government." These would include: (1) political stability, (2) sound bureaucracies based on meritocracy, (3) economic growth with equity, (4) fiscal prudence, and (5) relative lack of corruption. With these criteria in mind, it should be possible for multilateral institutions such as the World Bank to work out an operational definition that would determine eligibility for foreign aid.

The effect of such a reorientation of Western policies toward the Third World would be that less attention would be paid to the process by which Third World governments come into being and more attention would be paid to their performance. If their performance leads to serious and consistent improvement in the living conditions of the population, both the humanitarian and pragmatic considerations that underlie Western policies would be satisfied: the humanitarian because there would be less starvation and suffering, and the pragmatic because improving conditions would mean less migration to the West.

While human rights campaigns are often portrayed as an absolute moral good to be implemented without any qualifications, in practice Western governments are prudent and selective. For example, given their powerful vested interest in secure and stable oil supplies from Saudi Arabia, Western governments have not tried to export their standards of human rights or democracy to that country, for they know that any alternative to the stable rule of the Saudi government would very likely be bad for the West.

The recent Algerian experience introduces another complication for Western advocates of immediate democratization. Democracies work all too well in bringing out the true social and cultural face of a society. In Algeria the centuries-old Islamic heritage had been suppressed by the secular and modern values introduced by the post-colonial elite. That Islamic heritage is now surfacing, and it will probably surface in other Islamic societies that hold democratic elections. If these governments elected by popular mandate impose strict Islamic laws that restrict some human rights (as Iran has), should we respect their right to decide their own values and practices? There are no easy answers.

The reaction of the West to the military coup in Algeria illustrates the moral and political ambiguities. Officially, most Western governments have condemned the coup. However, the citizens of France, Italy, and Spain have questioned whether democracy in Algeria is good for their countries, and most Western governments have quietly welcomed the coup, taking a sensible, pragmatic position based on Western interests. In the eyes of many Third World observers this pragmatic application of moral values contributes to a cynical belief that the West will advance democracy only when it suits its own interests. The same cynicism can develop — is almost certain to develop — over human rights campaigns. Would the West be as tough on the Chinese regime in Beijing if China were located where either Turkey or Mexico is today? Would the West then be as sanguine about the prospect of millions of boat people emerging from China if the regime broke down and chaos prevailed?

Take the case of Peru. In Peru, as in Algeria, there was a spectacular reversal in the trend toward democratization. However, Peru was punished with sanctions, while Algeria was not. The Europeans wisely calculated that sanctions on Algeria would further destabilize the volatile socioeconomic situation and exacerbate the flow of Algerian refugees. Hence, nothing was done. Peru was farther away from any Western society. So, even though Peru's socioeconomic environment was just as volatile as Algeria's, and sanctions would be equally destabilizing, they were imposed.

Westerners should surely have asked what *kind* of authoritarian government Alberto Fujimori was imposing. Was he going to become a Ferdinand Marcos and enrich his personal coffers, or was he desperately trying to reverse course for a society on the verge of serious breakdown? Do such questions matter? Curiously, few have noticed that if *current* Western policies had been in force in the 1950s and 1960s the spectacular economic growth of Taiwan and South Korea could have been cut off at its very inception by the demand that the governments then in place be dismantled.

In Peru, one additional cause for concern is that if the sanctions succeed in their purpose of unseating the Fujimori government, the possible alternatives of chaos or a Latin American version of Pol Potism could be much worse for the Peruvian people. Those who firmly advocate sanctions on Peru should be prepared to accept moral responsibility for the consequences of those sanctions, good or bad. If they do so, the world may avoid a repetition of the Cambodian experience, where there were many voices advocating the removal of the Lon Nol regime, but no one accepted moral responsibility for the genocide that followed. If the West chooses to be prudent in targeting human rights abuses where its own interests are involved, does it not have an obligation to exercise the same prudence when others may be affected by these campaigns?

In the face of these moral and political complexities, Western governments may find it in their interest to explain to their citizens that prudence may have to be a crucial consideration in the promotion of human rights and democracy. Unfortunately, while Western governments are prudent in practice, they find it almost impossible to speak honestly to their own citizens on the subject. Philosophically, it is difficult to discuss prudence in promoting democratization; it is not an uplifting, inspirational virtue. Yet both honesty and self-interest suggest that Western governments should do so.

No Western government has publicly confessed that in determining its particular human rights and democracy policies it weighs them against other vital national interests, yet every government does so. The Germans take a strong stand on Kurdish rights, the United States does not. The United States and the United Kingdom come down hard on Mu'ammar Gadhafi, Italy does not. This pattern of inconsistencies in turn undervalues the merit of these human rights policies in the eyes of the ostensible beneficiaries, the Third World societies, because instead of being impressed by the moral courage of Western governments, they notice the pragmatic and calculated application of moral principles.

The human rights campaigns launched by Western governments and nongovernmental organizations have done much good. They have, for example, created a new global consensus that militates against the return of gross and egregious violators of human rights such as Pol Pot, Idi Amin, and Boukassa. The victims of such regimes can breathe a sigh of relief. Similarly, the strong global consensus against the gross forms of torture that prevailed in many parts of the world is a great advance in human history.

But from the viewpoint of many Third World citizens, human rights campaigns often have a bizarre quality. For many of them it looks something like this: They are like hungry and diseased passengers on a leaky, overcrowded boat that is about to drift into treacherous waters, in which many of them will perish. The captain of the boat is often harsh, sometimes fairly and sometimes not. On the riverbanks stand a group of affluent, well-fed, and well-intentioned onlookers. As soon as those onlookers witness a passenger being flogged or imprisoned or even deprived of his right to speak, they board the ship to intervene, protecting the passengers from the captain. But those passengers remain hungry and diseased. As soon as they try to swim to the banks into the arms of their benefactors, they are firmly returned to the boat, their primary sufferings unabated. This is no abstract analogy. It is exactly how the Haitians feel.

In the long run it may be wiser for the West to encourage a more viable process of transition in developing societies, one that puts the horse before the cart — promoting economic development through good government before promoting democracy. This is not to argue that the international community should tolerate vicious dictators, the Pol Pots or Idi Amins, as long as they promote economic development. Rather, Third World governments should be treated with the same degree of pragmatic realism as is already applied to the governments of Algeria, Morocco, and Tunisia by European governments.

Implementing this apparently simple reversal would be very difficult for most Western governments. Promoting democracy in most
cases involves little in the way of costs or sacrifices. But promoting economic development has significant costs, direct and indirect. What
may be good for the Third World in the long run (promoting economic
development first) could prove painful for Western societies in the
short run. The European community (EC) would, for example, need to
abandon its massive subsidies to inefficient European farmers. If the
West persists in taking the easy road in the short run, promoting
democracy first, it will ultimately prove painful and costly, because the
effects of massive Third World poverty and instability will appear on its
doorstep. Unfortunately, when there is a conflict between the short
term and the long term in democratic politics, it is usually safer to bet
that short-term considerations will prevail.

Western Democracy vs. Western Interests

The record of Western democracies in overcoming the various challenges they have faced is impressive. Unlike Athens, they have so far
triumphed in both peace and war. The resilience of these societies
should never be underestimated. Yet it is dangerous to assume that
they have no institutional defects.

In the absence of a clear and imminent threat, most Western governments find it difficult to convince their populations that, given the
seriousness of the post–Cold War challenges, they must be prepared to
accept some painful changes and sacrifices. The problem is not lack of
leadership in these societies, but institutional arrangements.

The global effects of these institutional defects of democracy can be
demonstrated with two examples, both of which have harmed the non-
Western world a great deal: the U.S. budget deficit and the EC Common
Agricultural Policy (CAP).

Despite a wide consensus in the United States that budget deficits
have to be stopped, the budget has effectively become a monster that
no government institution can effectively tame. Gramm-Rudman
failed miserably. The problem arises out of institutional defects in the
democratic system. The interlocking network of votes by the various

lobbies means that they have a stranglehold on the budget process, thereby guaranteeing the perpetuation of the enormous deficits.

Private lobbies distort the economic competitiveness of the United States in other ways, with ramifications that spill outside U.S. borders. For example, as far back as the early 1980s the U.S. auto industry asked for respite from Japanese competition and, through the intervention of the U.S. government, received it, in the form of voluntary restraints. In the decade that followed, instead of trying to learn from Japan and investing in competitiveness, the industry continued to pay both its shareholders and management rich dividends. No effort was made to check whether this public intervention was being used for public or private good. The Japanese government's intervention in the Japanese economy is done with the clear understanding that long-term Japanese national interests lie in enhancing, not undermining, the international competitiveness of Japanese industries. Not so in the United States, where government institutions respond to ad hoc pressures from private interests.

The Common Agricultural Policy is another monster that has been created out of the institutional defects of Western democracies. In private, virtually no EC leader can defend the CAP. In public, no French or Spanish or Italian leader would criticize it for fear of not being elected.

By absorbing more than two-thirds of the EC budget, the CAP draws funding away from industries that could enhance the EC's competitiveness. It has also crippled the General Agreement on Tarrifs and Trade (GATT) discussions because the non-EC nations see no reason why they should accept painful changes when the affluent EC nations will not do so. Why, for example, should Indonesia, Brazil, and Zaire — three nations that could form an "oxygen cartel" — curb their lucrative deforestation activities when the affluent EC societies will not accept any sacrifices? Only the lack of awareness of such problems can explain why the crippling of the Uruguay Round of GATT talks in December 1990 was allowed to happen by the West. This crippling seriously aggravated the new threats that the West faces in the post–Cold War era.

To prevent huge migrations from the poor to the affluent societies, a significant burst of economic development will be needed around the globe. One crucial global instrument that is needed to trigger such widespread economic development is GATT. If all societies abided by its rules, it would create a single and massive global marketplace that all societies, rich and poor, could plug in to. GATT has already demonstrated its power by carrying a significant portion of mankind — those living in the West — to the highest levels of comfort and affluence enjoyed in the history of man. It does this quite simply by creating a "level playing field" in which each society can exploit its comparative economic advantage. The impact on global productivity has been enormous.

There were few protests when the Uruguay Round was crippled in December 1990. Perhaps it was seen as merely a trade issue. The Brussels meeting failed, because the European Community wanted to protect certain industries from global competition. This will eventually prove futile, because capitalism is fundamentally a dynamic process. In trying to protect their industries from new competition, the West is trying to freeze an unfreezable process.

Given the historical impact it has already had and its relevance to the central problems of the immediate future, it is puzzling that more strategic thinkers have not focused on GATT. It is a mistake not to do so. By denying the vast masses an opportunity to improve their livelihood, a retreat from GATT to protectionism will force them to pound on the doors of the West.

Reorienting Western strategy in the post–Cold War era is a major task, requiring the sort of leadership that the United States so handsomely provided after World War II. Unfortunately, with the end of the Cold War the leadership of the West has fractured between the United States, Europe, and Japan at the very moment when the need for leadership in the Western world has never been greater. Unfortunately, too, Western societies are under strong pressure to turn inward when they should be looking outward. Having created a technology that has brought the world, with all of its attendant problems and promises, to its very doorstep, the West now has a strong impulse to shut the doors. This is a futile impulse, because the new technology has created a universe in which "interconnectedness" will be the order of the day.

The real danger is that the West will realize too late that — like the defenders of Singapore — it has been preoccupied with old challenges while new ones have been assuming massive proportions.

AN ASIAN PERSPECTIVE ON HUMAN RIGHTS AND FREEDOM OF THE PRESS

In January 1993 the Asia Society of New York and three Singapore institutions — the Institute of Southeast Asian Studies, the Singapore International Foundation, and the Institute of Policy Studies — organized the seminar "Asian and American Perspectives on Capitalism and Democracy" in Singapore. I was asked to give the Asian perspective on human rights and freedom of the press. James Fallows, my fellow panelist, was shocked and disturbed by my paper. I spelled out ten heresies, which I believed the West had either ignored or suppressed, and added five principles that could lead to a dialogue of equals between Asia and America. Since I touched on so many sacred cows, I assumed that Western journals, which love controversy, would want to publish it. However, none were interested until the Washington Quarterly *bravely published a shorter version entitled "Go East, Young Man." The longer version that follows has also been published in a collection of essays entitled* Debating Human Rights, *edited by Peter Van Ness.*

Clearly this is the angriest essay I have ever written. If I were writing it today I would not use the same tone. I made other mistakes: I quoted a Swiss economist who asserted that the U.S. government debt problem was beyond repair. In the intervening period, it has been repaired. Contrary to all expectations, the U.S. economy has flourished in the 1990s, and the Asian economies have stumbled. In many ways the world has changed.

But some hard realities have not changed. Most critically, the heresies I described in 1993 remain heresies today. The absolute power of the Western journalist in the Third World remains unchecked. Indeed, given the overwhelming power of the United States at the end of the century, the might of the American media has increased, not diminished. Within the

United States, there are informal checks and balances on this media power. Outside the United States, nothing restrains the American journalist.

If I may make another outrageous point, I would like to add that all this has led to huge distortion in Western perceptions of Asia. The only voices the Western media want to listen to are the voices of other Western journalists. Many write of Asia and Asians in a tone of condescension that speaks volumes about the need in the West to preserve certain caricatures of Asia. No level playing field yet exists in the journalistic world. That is why I believe that young Western students should still read this essay.

I WOULD LIKE TO BEGIN WITH AN ANALOGY, and I apologize to those who may have heard me recount it before:

> From the viewpoint of many Third World citizens, human rights campaigns often have a bizarre quality. For many of them it looks something like this: They are like hungry and diseased passengers on a leaky, overcrowded boat that is about to drift into treacherous waters, in which many of them will perish. The captain of the boat is often harsh, sometimes fairly and sometimes not. On the riverbanks stand a group of affluent, well-fed, and well-intentioned onlookers. As soon as those onlookers witness a passenger being flogged or imprisoned or even deprived of his right to speak, they board the ship to intervene, protecting the passengers from the captain. But those passengers remain hungry and diseased. As soon as they try to swim to the banks into the arms of their benefactors, they are firmly returned to the boat, their primary sufferings unabated. This is no abstract analogy. It is exactly how the Haitians feel.[1]

This is just one of the many absurd aspects of the aggressive Western promotion of human rights at the end of the Cold War. There are many others. Yet, when I tried in seminars at Harvard University to challenge the universal applicability of democracy, human rights, or freedom of the press, I discovered that these values have become virtual "sacred cows." No one could challenge their intrinsic worth. Worse still, when I persisted, I was greeted with sniggers, smug looks, and general derision. The general assumption there was that any Asian, especially a Singaporean, who challenged these concepts was doing so only in an attempt to cover up the sins of his government.

I am as convinced now as I was then that the aggressive Western promotion of democracy, human rights, and freedom of the press to the Third World at the end of the Cold War was, and is, a colossal mistake. This campaign is unlikely to benefit the 4.3 billion people who live outside the developed world, and perhaps not even the 700 million people who live inside it. This campaign could aggravate, rather than ameliorate, the difficult conditions under which the vast majority of the world's population lives.

But to get this central point into Western minds, one must first remove the barriers that have made these topics into untouchable sacred cows in Western discourse. A Westerner must first acknowledge that when he discusses these topics with a non-Westerner, he is, consciously or unconsciously, standing behind a pulpit. If it is any consolation, let me hasten to add that this attitude is not new. As the following passage from the *Dictionary of the History of Ideas* indicates, it goes back centuries.

> The concept of despotism began as a distinctively European perception of Asian governments and practices: Europeans as such were considered to be free by nature, in contrast to the servile nature of the Orientals. Concepts of despotism have frequently been linked to justifications, explanations, or arraignments of slavery, conquest, and colonial or imperial domination. The attribution of despotism to an enemy may be employed to mobilize the members of a political unit, or those of a regional area. Thus the Greeks stigmatized the Persians as despotic in much the same way that Christian writers were to treat the Turks. By an irony not always perceived either by the purported champions of liberty against despotism, or by their historians, such arguments often became the rationale, as in Aristotle, for the domination by those with a tradition of liberty over others who had never enjoyed that happy condition.[2]

On the eve of the twenty-first century, this European attitude toward Asians must end; the assumption of moral superiority must be abandoned. A level playing field needs to be created for meaningful discussions between Asians and Americans. That will be my first goal in this paper. In the second half I will put across the view of one Asian on human rights and freedom of the press.

A Level Playing Field

It is never a pleasant experience to be lowered from a pedestal. I apologize for any psychological discomfort that my remarks may cause. Yet, to achieve this objective in one paper, I will have to be ruthless if I am to be brief. To remove the "sacred cow" dimension surrounding the subjects of human rights and freedom of the press, I propose to list ten heresies that the West, including the United States, has either ignored, suppressed, or treated as irrelevant or inconsequential in its discussions on these subjects. If these heresies have any validity at all, I hope that this will lead Western writers to accept that they do not have a monopoly on wisdom or virtue of these subjects and that they should try to exercise a little more humility when they discourse on these subjects to a non-Western audience.

Heresy No. 1: American journalists do not believe in the Christian rule "Do unto others as you would have others do unto you."
From Gary Hart to Bill Clinton there has developed an honorable journalistic tradition that the marital infidelities of a politician are public property to be exposed in every detail. But those who participate in this tradition do not feel themselves bound by Jesus Christ's statement "Let him who has not sinned cast the first stone."

To the best of my limited knowledge, based on my short stay in Washington, D.C., the level of infidelities seemed about the same in all sectors of society, whether in Congress or in the press corps. Power proves to be a great aphrodisiac. Both politicians and journalists have equal difficulty resisting the temptations that flow their way. Yet the actions of one group are deemed immoral and subject to public scrutiny, while those of the other are deemed private matters. But in the informal pecking order worked out in Washington (as in any other tribal society), many a senior journalist enjoys far more effective power than a congressman. But they are subject to different levels of scrutiny.

The same disparity applies to personal finances. All aspiring politicians, even the few unfortunate ones who may have entered politics to do a service to the nation, have to declare every penny of their financial worth. Yet none of the Washington journalists, many of whom enjoy far greater incomes, feel any moral obligation to declare all their financial worth; nor do they feel any need to declare how their own financial worth would be enhanced by discussing the financial worth of an aspiring politician. A full disclosure of income and wealth on the part of those who make and those who influence public policy decisions (including lobbyists and journalists) will probably indicate the great mismatch in financial muscle between the actual policymakers and those who seek to influence them. It may also help to illuminate why, despite so many rational discussions, so many irrational public policy choices are made.

Heresy No. 2: Power corrupts. The absolute power of the Western journalist in the Third World corrupts absolutely.

The greatest myth that a journalist cherishes is that he is an underdog: the lone ranger who works against monstrous bureaucracies to uncover the real truth, often at great personal risk. I never understood this myth when I was in Washington. Cabinet secretaries, senators and congressmen, ambassadors, and generals promptly returned the phone calls of, and assiduously cultivated, the Washington journalists. Not all these powerful office-holders were as good as Kissinger or Jim Baker at seducing American journalists, but none would dare tell an American journalist of a major paper to go to hell. It would be as inconceivable as trying to exercise dissent in the court of Attila the Hun. Yet the myth persists that the journalist is at a disadvantage.

The cruelest results of this myth are experienced in the developing world. An American journalist arriving in a Third World capital brings with him, as a deeply embedded unconscious preconception, the belief that he is a lone ranger battling an evil and corrupt Third World government. Never would he admit that he arrives in a Third World capital with as much power as a colonial proconsul in the nineteenth century. The host government ignores such emissaries at its own peril. The average correspondent from an influential Western journal who arrives in a Third World capital asks to see the president, prime minister, and perhaps foreign minister. If, heaven forbid, any of these leaders should refuse, this would be a typical response: "Given that kings and presidents throughout the world regularly grant interviews to the *Guardian* (please note our recent exclusive interview with the King of Jordan) and, indeed, sometimes write in the *Guardian* (as with former President Gorbachev), I do wonder by what token the *Guardian* is not considered worthy of such a request. We are, after all, the second-highest-selling quality national daily in the UK." (Note: this is an extract from an actual letter.)

A Western journalist would be thoroughly puzzled by a request for reciprocity from, say, a journalist from the *Times of India* in Washington, D.C. Pressed for a justification for this imbalance, he would dismiss the case for reciprocity on the grounds that the *New York Times*, for example, is a better paper than the *Times of India*. Never would he admit to himself that the prime minister, even of India, would hesitate to turn down a request by the *New York Times*, because that paper controls the gateways to key minds in Washington. What is sweet about this exercise of power by a *Times* correspondent is that he would never have to admit that he was savoring the delicious fruits of power, since they come with no obvious trappings of office.

Heresy No. 3: A free press can serve as the opium of society.
This statement is not quite as outrageous as Marx's dictum that religion is the opium of the people, but it will probably be dismissed as quickly as Marx's statement was when he first uttered it. The American media pride themselves on the ability of their investigative journalism to uncover the real truth behind the stories put out by government, big business, and other major institutions. They could never stomach the proposition that they serve as the opium of American society. But they do.

In the past twenty years there have been two parallel developments. First, American journalism has become much more aggressive than it ever was. Kennedy was the last U.S. president to be treated with kid gloves; his sexual excesses were well known but not publicized. Since then no U.S. president has been considered off-limits for total coverage, giving the impression that the U.S. government is under total and close scrutiny.

The parallel trend is this. The past twenty years have also seen increasingly bad government. Lyndon Johnson felt that he could fight a war and create a good society without raising taxes. This began the process of fiscal indiscipline. Richard Nixon's flaws are well known, as are Jimmy Carter's. In the past twelve years, under two Republican administrations, the United States has gone from being the world's largest creditor country to being the world's largest debtor country. A Swiss investment consultant, Jean Antoine Cramer, noted recently, "It took 150 years for the U.S. government to create a debt of $1000bn, and only 10 years to quadruple this debt. With a GNP of $5600bn, the situation is beyond repair. American consumers owe $7000bn, corporations $5000bn and the government $5000bn." No American politician, in the land of the free press, dares to utter any hard truths on the sacrifices needed to stop this rot. The consequence has been irresponsible government on a mind-boggling and historically unparalleled scale. Equally striking are the parallel troubles of some of the largest U.S. corporations, including names such as the previously blue-chip Citicorp, GM, and IBM, all of which have also been under close scrutiny by the press.

It would be impossible for me, even if I had the whole day, to prove that there is a causal connection between a more aggressive free press and increasingly bad government. It may be pure coincidence. After all, the U.S. press has been second to none in exposing the follies of the U.S. government. But have all their exposures served as opiates, creating the illusion that something is being done when really nothing is being done?

There may be an even more cruel example of the free press serving as an opiate. One of the post–World War II achievements that the United States is very proud of is the political emancipation of African Americans. The press played a key role in this. But did the reporting of this apparent emancipation foster the illusion that the fundamental problems of the African Americans had been solved? The impression given was that equality had finally been achieved by the African Americans. The doors had been opened. All they had to do was walk through.

Thirty years after the famous civil rights marches, if one were to ask an average African American family, "Are you better off than you were thirty years ago?" how many would say yes and how many would say no? What did the large-scale rioting after the Rodney King episode demonstrate? That perhaps thirty years of discussion of African Americans' problems have served as a substitute for thirty years of action, creating an illusion of movement when there has been little or none. Is it enough for the U.S. media to say, "We did the best we can"? Or should they begin to ask, "Did we contribute to this failure in any way?"

Can the minds generated by the freest press in the world conceive of such questions?

Heresy No. 4: A free press does not necessarily lead to a well-ordered society. A key assumption in the West is that a good society needs a free press to keep abuses of power in check, that freedom of information checks bad government, and that its absence leads to greater abuses and bad government.

These statements may well be true. A free press can certainly contribute to good government. But the opposite may also be true. A free press can also lead to bad government.

In Southeast Asia we have seen an unfortunate demonstration of this. The one country in Southeast Asia that has enjoyed the freest press, by far, for the longest period of time (except for the Marcos martial law interregnum) is the Philippines. But the Philippines is also the Association of Southeast Asian Nations (ASEAN) society that is having the greatest difficulty in modernization and economic progress, suggesting that a free press is neither a necessary nor a sufficient condition for development and progress.

India and China provide two massive social laboratories to judge what prescriptions would help a society develop and prosper. Between them, they hold about two-fifths of the world's population — two out of every five human beings on the planet. Each has taken a very different political road. The West approves the freedom of the press in India, frowns on the lack of it in China. Yet which society is developing faster today, and which society is likely to modernize first?

The recent Ayodhya incident demonstrated one important new dimension for societies all around the globe. The Indian media tried to control emotional reactions by restricting the broadcasting and distribution of video scenes of the destruction of the mosque. But now many Indian homes can see video clips (transmitted through satellites and tapes) from foreign news agencies, which felt no reason to exercise social, political, or moral restraint. Those who happily transmitted the video clips never had to bear the consequences themselves. They were sitting comfortably in Atlanta, Georgia, or Hong Kong while the riots that followed in India as a result of their TV transmissions never reached their homes. Unfortunately these media personnel did not stop to consider whether they could have saved other human lives, not their own, by exercising restraint.

Heresy No. 5: Western journalists, in covering non-Western events, are conditioned by both Western prejudices and Western interests. The claim of "objective" reporting is a major falsehood.

Let me cite three major examples. First, the coverage of Islam. Edward W. Said, in his book *Covering Islam*, states:

> The hardest thing to get most academic experts on Islam to admit is that what they say and do as scholars is set in a profoundly and in some ways an offensively political context. Everything about the study of Islam in the contemporary West is saturated with political importance, but hardly any writers on Islam, whether expert or general, admit the fact in what they say. Objectivity is assumed to inhere in learned discourse about other societies, despite the long history of political, moral, and religious concern felt in all societies, Western or Islamic, about the alien, the strange and different. In Europe, for example, the Orientalist has traditionally been affiliated directly with colonial offices: what we have just begun to learn about the extent of close cooperation between scholarship and direct military colonial conquest (as in the case of revered Dutch

Orientalist C. Snouck Hurgronje, who used the confidence he had won from Muslims to plan and execute the brutal Dutch war against the Atjehnese people of Sumatra) is both edifying and depressing. Yet books and articles continue to pour forth extolling the nonpolitical nature of Western scholarship, the fruits of Orientalist learning, and the value of "objective" expertise. At the very same time there is scarcely an expert on "Islam" who has not been a consultant or even an employee of the government, the various corporations, the media. My point is that the cooperation must be admitted and taken into account, not just for moral reasons, but for intellectual reasons as well.[3]

Second, the U.S. media coverage of the Vietnam War, a major event, some say a glorious chapter, in the history of U.S. journalism. By the late 1960s and early 1970s, as American bodies were brought back from Vietnam, American public sentiment turned against the war. The United States had to get out. The U.S. media helped to manufacture a justification: that the United States was supporting the "bad guys" (the crooked and wicked Saigon and Phnom Penh regimes) against the "good guys" (the dedicated, incorruptible revolutionaries in North Vietnam or the Cambodian jungles). Books such as *Fire in the Lake*, a glorification of the Vietnamese revolution, became the Bible of American reporters. When the last American soldier left Vietnam, most American journalists felt satisfied and vindicated.

The subsequent Communist victories in Cambodia and Vietnam exposed the true nature of the revolutionaries. The story of the Cambodian genocide is well known, as is the story of the thousands of boat people who perished in the South China Sea. The level of human misery increased, not decreased, after the revolution. Yet virtually no American journalist came forward to admit that perhaps he had been wrong in quoting from *Fire in the Lake* or in calling for the abandonment of the Saigon and Phnom Penh regimes. As long as American journalists had fulfilled vital U.S. interests by saving American lives, they did not feel there was any need for them to weigh the moral consequences of their actions on non-Americans — the Vietnamese or the Cambodians.

Third, the coverage of the events in Tiananmen Square, which became a global media focus. The essential Western media story described a revolution by Chinese democrats against Chinese autocrats. The replica of the Statue of Liberty appeared on TV screens constantly to provide the pictorial image for this. Yet for all their massive coverage of Tiananmen, the Western media failed to explain how this event was seen through Chinese eyes. Few Chinese intellectuals believe that China is ready for democracy. Most are as afraid of chaos and anarchy (a persistent Chinese disease) as they are of a return to Maoist totalitarianism. The Tiananmen Square incidents were a battle between soft authoritarians and hard authoritarians. The Western media vividly reported the apparent victory of the "hard-liners," but they failed to tell the world the true aftermath: the soft authoritarians have come back to power.

During Tiananmen several Western journalists were blatantly dishonest. They would lunch with a student on a "hunger strike" before reporting on his "hunger." They were not all bystanders reporting on an event; several advised the students how to behave. None stayed to deal with the consequences that the students had to face.

A telling indication of how American journalists are affected by U.S. interests in their reporting on China is to compare 1970s publications with those of the early 1990s. When Nixon landed in China in 1972 the U.S. media had a virtual love-fest with a regime that had just killed millions in the Cultural Revolution. Yet in the 1990s a much more benign Chinese government, which has liberated millions from poverty and indignity and promises to launch them on the road to development, is treated as a pariah regime.

Heresy No. 6: Western governments work with genocidal rulers when it serves their interests to do so.

It was August 1942, a dark moment in World War II. Churchill had flown secretly to Moscow to bring some bad news personally to Stalin: the Allies were not ready for a second front in Europe. Stalin reacted angrily. Nancy Caldwell Sorel, describing that meeting, writes:

Discord continued, but on the last evening, when Churchill went to say goodbye, Stalin softened . . . the hour that Churchill had planned for extended to seven. Talk and wine flowed freely, and in a moment of rare intimacy, Stalin admitted that even the stresses of war did not compare to the terrible struggle to force the collective farm policy on the peasantry. Millions of Kulaks had been, well, eliminated. The historian Churchill thought of Burke's dictum "If I cannot have reform without justice, I will not have reform," but the politician Churchill concluded that with the war requiring unity, it was best not to moralize aloud.[4]

The story elicits a chuckle. What a shrewd old devil Churchill was. How cunning of him not to displease Stalin with moralizing. Neither then nor now has Churchill's reputation been sullied by his association with a genocidal ruler. Now change the cast of characters to an identical set: Margaret Thatcher and Pol Pot. Historically they could have met, but of course they never did. Now try to describe a possible meeting and try to get a chuckle out of it. Impossible? Why?

Think about it. Think hard, for in doing so you will discover to your surprise that it is possible for thoughtful and well-informed people to have double standards. If the rule that prevents any possible meeting between Margaret Thatcher and Pol Pot is "Thou shalt not have any discourse with a genocidal ruler," then the same rule also forbids any meeting between Stalin and Churchill. Moral rules, as the English philosopher R. M. Hare has stressed, are inherently universalizable. If we do want to allow a meeting between Churchill and Stalin (since, until the past few weeks, no historian has ever condemned Churchill, that must be the prevailing sentiment), then the rule has to be modified to "Thou shalt not have any discourse with a genocidal ruler, unless there are mitigating circumstances."

This is not a mere change of nuance. We have made a fundamental leap, a leap best understood by the analogy contained in the following tale. A man meets a woman and asks her whether she would spend the night with him for a million dollars. She replies, "For a million dollars, sure."

He says, "How about five dollars?"

She replies indignantly, "What do you think I am?"

He replies, "We have already established what you are. We are only negotiating the price."

All those who condone Churchill's meeting with Stalin but would readily condemn any meeting with Pol Pot belong in the woman's shoes (logically speaking).

In Stalin's case, as England's survival was at stake, all was excused. In Pol Pot's case, as no conceivable vital Western interest could be served in any meeting with him, no mitigating excuse could possibly exist. Hence the total and absolute Western condemnation of any contact with Pol Pot or his minions in the Khmer Rouge. The tragedy for the Cambodian people is that the West, in applying this absolute moral rule only because its own vital interests were not involved, did not stop to ask whether the sufferings of the Cambodians could have been mitigated if the West had been as flexible in its dealings with the Khmer Rouge as Churchill was with Stalin.

Throughout the 1980s, when several Asian governments were trying to achieve a viable Cambodian peace settlement (which would invariably have to include the Khmer Rouge), they were vilified for their direct contacts with the Khmer Rouge. American diplomats were instructed never to shake hands with Khmer Rouge representatives.

In the past twelve months the atrocities committed by Radovan Karadzic and his Serbian followers (in full view of the U.S. media) should be sufficient justification to put them in the same league as Pol Pot or Idi Amin. Yet no Western diplomat has hesitated to shake the hands of these Serbian representatives. Is there one standard for Westerners and another for Asians?

Heresy No. 7: Western governments will happily sacrifice the human rights of Third World societies when it suits Western interests to do so.

The regime in Myanmar overturned the results of the democratic elections in 1990 and brutally suppressed the popular demonstrations that followed. Myanmar was punished with Western sanctions. Asian governments were criticized for not enthusiastically following suit.

The regime in Algeria overturned the results of the democratic elections in 1992 and brutally suppressed the popular demonstrations that followed. Algeria was not punished with Western sanctions. The Asian governments have never been provided with an explanation for this obvious double standard.

But the reasons are obvious. The fear of Western sanctions triggering off greater political instability, leading to thousands of boat people crossing the tiny Mediterranean Sea into Europe, made the EC governments prudent and cautious. Despite this, they had no hesitation in criticizing Asian governments for exercising the same prudence for the same reasons when it came to applying sanctions against Myanmar or China. Double standards, by any criterion, are obviously immoral. How many Western papers have highlighted this?

Heresy No. 8: The West has used the pretext of human rights abuses to abandon Third World allies that no longer serve Western interests.
The "sins" of Mohammed Siad Barre (Somalia), Mobutu Sese Seko (Zaire), and Daniel Arap Moi (Kenya) were as well known during the Cold War as they are now. They did not convert from virtue to vice the day the Cold War ended. Yet behavior that was deemed worthy of Western support during the Cold War was deemed unacceptable when the Cold War ended.

It is remarkable how much satisfaction the Western governments, media, and public have expressed over their ability finally to pursue "moral" policies now that the Cold War has ended. Yet they have made no admission that the West was (logically speaking) pursuing immoral policies during the Cold War. Nor has anyone addressed the question of whether it is honorable to use and abandon allies.

Heresy No. 9: The West cannot acknowledge that the pursuit of "moral" human rights policies can have immoral consequences.
At the end of the Paris International Conference on Cambodia (ICC) in August 1989, the then Vietnamese foreign minister Nguyen Co Thach, insisted that the conference declaration should call for a nonreturn of the genocidal policies and practices of the Khmer Rouge. All present knew

that Nguyen Co Thach was not really concerned about Pol Pot's record. (Indeed, Thach once made the mistake of privately confessing to congressman Stephen Solarz that Vietnam did not invade Cambodia to save the Cambodian people from Pol Pot, even though this was the official Vietnamese propaganda line.) However, Thach knew that the Khmer Rouge, a party to the Paris conference, would not accept such a reference. Hence, the conference would fail, a failure that the Vietnamese wanted, because they were not ready then to relinquish control of Cambodia. Western officials did not dare to challenge him for fear that Nguyen Co Thach would expose them to their own media. At the same time, despite having scuttled a conference that could have brought peace to Cambodia, Nguyen Co Thach came out looking good in the eyes of the Western media, because he had taken a strong stand against the Khmer Rouge. Yet in practical terms, from the viewpoint of the ordinary Cambodian, the strong Western consensus against the Khmer Rouge had backfired, hurting the Cambodians, because it prevented the Western delegations from exposing Nguyen Co Thach's blatant scuttling of the peace conference. Out of good (the Western media's condemnation of Pol Pot) came evil (the destruction of a peace conference). This was not the first time it had happened in history. As Max Weber said in his famous essay "Politics as a Vocation," "It is *not* true that good can only follow from good and evil only from evil, but that often the opposite is true. Anyone who says this is, indeed, a political infant."[5]

The morally courageous thing for a Western delegate to have done at that Paris conference would have been to stand up in front of the Western media and explain why the inclusion of the Khmer Rouge was necessary if one wanted a peace agreement that would end the Cambodians' sufferings. No Western leader even dreamed of doing so, so strong was the sentiment against the Khmer Rouge. This produced a curious contradiction for moral philosophers: the ostensibly morally correct position (that is, of excluding the Khmer Rouge) produced an immoral result — the prolonging of the Cambodians' agony.

This was not by any means the first of such moral dilemmas confronted by Western officials. Max Weber asserts, "No ethics in the world can dodge the fact that in numerous instances the attainment of 'good' ends is bound to the fact that one must be willing to pay the price of using morally dubious means or at least dangerous ones."[6] Unfortunately there is no living Western statesman who has the courage to make such a statement, for in the era of "political correctness" that we live in, the Western media would excoriate any such brave soul. Out of moral correctness we have produced moral cowardice.

Heresy No. 10: An imperfect government that commits some human rights violations is better than no government, in many societies.

At least two nation-states have broken apart since the end of the Cold War — Somalia and Yugoslavia. Both shared a common characteristic of being useful to the West during the Cold War. The sins of their governments were forgiven then. When these ruling regimes were abandoned (each in a different way), the net result was an increase in human misery. A utilitarian moral philosopher would have no difficulty arguing that the previous situation of imperfect government was a better moral choice, because it caused less misery.

The inability of the West to accept this will lead to the same result in other countries. Take Peru, for example. It was drifting toward chaos and anarchy. President Fujimori imposed emergency rule to halt the slide. He should have been praised for his courage in taking decisive action to prevent anarchy. However, because the form of his action, a temporary retreat from parliamentary rule, was deemed unacceptable by the West, the beneficial consequences of his action for the Peruvian people were ignored by the West. In trying to maintain its form of ideological purity, the West was prepared to sacrifice the interests of the Peruvian people.

If the current Western policy of punishing authoritarian governments had been in force in the 1960s and 1970s, the spectacular economic growth of Taiwan and South Korea would have been cut off at its very inception by Western demands that the governments then in power be replaced by less authoritarian regimes. Instead, by allowing the authoritarian governments, which were fully committed to economic development, to run the full course, the West has brought about the very economic and social changes that have paved the way for the more open and participative societies that Taiwan and South Korea have become. The lessons from East Asia are clear. There are no short-cuts. It is necessary for a developing society to first succeed in economic development before it can attain the social and political freedoms enjoyed by developed societies.

There is no unified Asian view on human rights and freedom of the press. These are Western concepts. Asians are obliged to react to them. Predictably, there is a whole range of reactions, from those who subscribe to these concepts in toto to those who reject them completely. An understanding of the Asian reactions is clouded by the fact that many Asians feel obliged to pay at least lip service to Western values. For example, many Japanese intellectuals, who remain children of the Meiji Restoration in their belief that Japan should become more Western than Asian, proclaim their adherence to Western values on human rights although they have a curious inability to discuss Japan's record in World War II in the same breath. From New Delhi to Manila, to name just two cities, there are many strong believers in these values. But in most Asian societies there is little awareness, let alone understanding, of these concepts. The truth is that the vast continent of Asia, preoccupied with more immediate challenges, has not had the time or energy to address these issues squarely.

I shall, therefore, make no pretense of speaking on behalf of Asia, although I am reasonably confident that my views will not be dismissed as eccentric by most Asians. My hope today is to find some credible middle ground where Asians and Americans can have a dialogue as equals who hold equally legitimate points of view. I will be so bold as to venture five principles that should guide such a discourse.

Principle No. 1: Mutual respect
The first principle that I want to stress is that all discussions between Asians and Americans on the subject of human rights and freedom of the press should be based on mutual respect. I have visited the offices of four great American newspapers: the *New York Times*, the *Washington Post*, the *Los Angeles Times*, and the *Wall Street Journal*. In any one of the four offices, if you ventured out at night and strayed a

few hundred yards off course, you would be putting your life in jeopardy. Yet, despite this, none of the editorial desks or writers would argue in favor of the reduction of the civil liberties of habitual criminals. Danger from habitual crime is considered an acceptable price to pay for no reduction in liberty. This is one social choice.

In Singapore you can wander out at night in any direction from the *Straits Times* office and not put your life in jeopardy. One reason for this is that habitual criminals and drug addicts are locked up, often for long spells, until they clearly have been reformed. The interest of the majority in having safe city streets is put ahead of considerations of rigorous due process, although safeguards are put in place to ensure that innocent individuals are not locked up. This is another kind of social choice. Let me suggest that neither is intrinsically superior. Let those who make the choice live with the consequences of their choice. Similarly, if this statement can be received without the usual Western sniggers, let me add that a city that bans the sale of chewing gum has as much moral right to do so as a city that effectively allows the sale of crack on its streets. Let us try to avoid the knee-jerk smug response that one choice is more moral than the other.

I do not want to belabor this point, but it will be psychologically difficult for the West to accept the notion that alternative social and political choices can deserve equal respect. For five hundred years the West has been dominant in one form or another. After World War II most of Asia, like much of the Third World, was politically emancipated. But the process of mental emancipation, on the part of the colonizers as much as the colonized, is taking much longer. This explains why Chris Patten can march into Hong Kong five years before its date of return to China and suggest a form of government that is completely unacceptable to China. The British would be shocked if a Chinese governor were to arrive in Northern Ireland and dictate terms for its liberation from the United Kingdom. But they see nothing absurd in what they are doing in Hong Kong. The British, like many in the West, feel that they have a right to dictate terms to Asians.

Eventually, as East Asia becomes more affluent, the discussions will take place on a basis of equality. But forums such as ours can anticipate this by trying to create a form of discourse in which we approach each other with mutual respect.

Principle No. 2: Economic development

The fundamental concern of Western proponents of human rights is to remove egregious abuses and improve the living conditions of the 4.3 billion people who live outside the developed world. Let me suggest that the current Western campaign (even if it is rigorously carried out, which is unlikely) will make barely a dent on the lives of the 4.3 billion people, although there will be symbolic victories such as the Aquino revolution or the award of the Nobel Peace Prize to Aung San Suu Kyi.

There is only one force that has the power to "liberate" the Third World. Economic development is probably the most subversive force created in history. It shakes up old social arrangements and paves the way for the participation of a greater percentage of society in social and political decisions. The Chinese Communist Party can no longer regain the tight totalitarian control it enjoyed in Mao Zedong's time. Deng Xiaoping's reforms have killed that possibility. Hence, if the West wants to bury forever Mao's totalitarian arrangements, it should support Deng's reforms to the hilt, even if he has to occasionally crack down to retain political control. The fundamental trend is clear. It is, therefore, not surprising that three and a half years after Tiananmen it is the "soft" and not the "hard" authoritarians who are in charge in Beijing. Clearly, if the Clinton administration wants to fulfill its goal of moving China toward a greater respect for human rights, it should do all in its power to accelerate China's economic development, not retard it.

Unfortunately the promotion of economic development (unlike the promotion of democracy and human rights) is difficult. It has significant costs, direct and indirect, for developed societies. What may be good for the Third World (promoting economic development) would prove painful for Western societies in the short run. The EC, the United States, and Japan, for example, would have to abandon their massive agricultural subsidies. Unfortunately (and paradoxically) the very nature of Western democratic societies (which inhibits politicians from speaking about sacrifices) may well be one of the biggest barriers to the effective spread of democracy and human rights in the Third World, including Asia.

Principle No. 3: Work with existing governments.
Westerners should not even dream of overthrowing most of the existing governments in Asia. I say this because I was present at a lynching at Harvard University, the lynching of the Indonesian government. This was at a forum organized at the Kennedy School of Government to discuss the unfortunate killings in Dili in November 1991. Two of the American journalists who had had a close shave in the incident were there to present vivid firsthand accounts and whip the crowd into a frenzy, with the help of a few leftist critics of the Indonesian government. This left a hapless State Department official to explain why the United States should continue working with the Suharto government. If the people in that room had had the power to depose the Indonesian government, they would have done it instantly, without paying a thought to the horrendous consequences that might follow. This is the attitude of many human rights activists: get rid of the imperfect governments we know — do not worry about the consequences that may follow. On their own, such activists will probably cause little trouble. But when they get into positions of influence, their ability to cause real damage increases by leaps and bounds.

In dealing with Asia I am calling on the United States to take the long view. These are societies that have been around hundreds, if not thousands, of years. They cannot be changed overnight, even if, for example, Fang Lizhi is elected president of China. The experience of President Aquino should provide a vivid lesson to those who believe that one change at the top can reform everything.

At its present stage of development, Asia needs governments that are committed to rapid economic development. Fortunately there are quite a few, ranging across a wide political spectrum, from the communist societies of China and Vietnam to the military-dominated societies of Thailand, and Indonesia and the democratic societies of South Korea, Taiwan, and Malaysia. All are experiencing rapid economic growth. They should be rewarded and encouraged (if only to act as models for others). Sporadic instances of political crackdowns should be criticized, but these governments should not be penalized as long as their people's lives are improving. Only societies such as North Korea and Myanmar, which have let their people stagnate for decades, deserve such disapproval.

Principle No. 4: Establish minimal codes of civilized conduct.
To a Western human rights activist, the suggestion that he should be a *little* moderate in making human rights demands on non-Western societies seems almost as absurd as the notion that a woman can be a little bit pregnant. In psychological attitudes, such an activist is no different from the religious crusaders of the past. He demands total conversion, nothing else. Such zealots can do a lot of damage. Unfortunately, since they occupy the high moral ground in Western societies, no government or media representative dares to challenge them openly. But some of the demands of these human rights activists would be unacceptable under any conditions. Most Asian societies would be shocked by the sight of gay-rights activists on their streets. And in most of them, if popular referendums were held, they would vote overwhelmingly in favor of the death penalty as well as censorship of pornography.

However, both Asians and Americans are human beings. They can agree on minimal standards of civilized behavior that both would like to live by. For example, there should be no torture, no slavery, no arbitrary killings, no disappearances in the middle of the night, no shooting down of innocent demonstrators, no imprisonment without careful review. These rights should be upheld not only for moral reasons. There are sound functional reasons. Any society that is at odds with its best and brightest and shoots them down when they demonstrate peacefully, as Myanmar did, is headed for trouble. Most Asian societies do not want to be in the position that Myanmar is in today, a nation at odds with itself.

Principle No. 5: Let the free press fly on its own wings.
Finally, on the difficult issue of the freedom of the press, let me suggest that neither the West in general nor the United States in particular

should take on the self-appointed role of guardian of free press in societies around the globe. Let each society decide for itself whether it would help or hinder its development if it decided to have a free press.

I have yet to meet an American who has any doubts about the virtues of having a free press. Even those who despise most journalists as the scum of the earth would not have it any other way. The value of the freedom of the press is treated as absolute, beyond challenge. The paradox here is that while they believe the virtues of a free press to be self-evident, they have no hesitation about ramming the concept down the throats of societies that are not enamored of it.

Over time a Darwinian process will establish whether societies with a free press will outperform those without one. So far, the record of the twentieth century shows that societies that have free newspapers, such as the *New York Times* or the *Washington Post*, have outperformed societies with *Pravda* and *Izvestia*. This winning streak may well continue. And if it does, more and more societies will naturally gravitate to social and political systems that can handle a totally free press, in the belief and hope that they will join the league of winners in the Darwinian contest between societies.

But let these decisions be made autonomously by these societies. There need be no fear that they will remain ignorant of the virtues of the U.S. media. The globe is shrinking. With the proliferation of satellite dishes in villages in India and Indonesia, the sky is shrinking too. CNN and BBC are available worldwide. The *International Herald Tribune* and the *Wall Street Journal* can be obtained practically anywhere around the globe. Let the merits of these papers speak for themselves. The U.S. media should not resort to the strong arm of the U.S. executive branch or Congress to sell their virtues for them.

In short, live and let live. If the United States is convinced that its systems of human rights and freedom of the press are the best possible systems for any society around the globe, let the virtues of these systems speak for themselves. As in the world of ideas, if a social system has merit, it will fly on its own wings. If it does not, it will not. Most Asians now know enough about these systems to make their own choices. Let them do so in peace.

POL POT: THE PARADOX
OF MORAL CORRECTNESS

It is a historical curiosity that Cambodia, a country of seven million people, could produce one of the evil giants of the twentieth century, almost on par with Hitler and Stalin. When the Vietnamese army removed Pol Pot from power in December 1978, the world applauded. But when the Vietnamese decided to remain in Cambodia as an army of invasion and occupation, an acute moral dilemma was created: whether or not to work with Pol Pot, whose help might be needed to remove the Vietnamese occupation. Most Cambodians and Southeast Asians chose to work with Pol Pot for the same reasons that Churchill had chosen to work with Stalin against Hitler, but every major Western newspaper and journal condemned the partnership. This essay tries to spell out the paradoxically harmful consequences of such morally correct postures that were the fashion among Western intellectuals in the 1980s. Significantly, such moral correctness dissipated when Western intellectuals had to cope directly with morally complex situations in places such as Bosnia and Chechnya. Still, I was surprised no Western op-ed guru dared to articulate the views suggested in this essay — published originally in Terrorism *in 1993.*

In the summer of 2000 I had an opportunity to visit Cambodia after twenty-six years. It still remains a poor society, scarred by the legacy of many wars. But the period during which I returned to Cambodia was probably one of the most peaceful and stable moments Cambodia has experienced in three decades. It was heartwarming to see so many ordinary folks trying to rebuild their lives after experiencing so many horrors.

The story of Cambodia has had no fairy-tale ending. Hun Sen gained effective authority over Cambodia following a brief fractious military struggle in mid-1997. The institutions of democracy have not been planted.

The difficult question of putting former Khmer Rouge leaders on trial continues to haunt the country. Much can be criticized in Cambodia, but the imperfect situation that the country enjoys in 2000 may be the best possible situation for most of its residents.

All this will not satisfy Western human rights activists who want to settle old scores and have a complete changing of the guard in Cambodia. In an ideal world this might be feasible. But set against the backdrop of thirty years of war and terror, the present imperfect situation seems almost idyllic. The old paradox about the dangers of not working with the Khmer Rouge to liberate Cambodia have been replaced with a new paradox: that the search for perfect solutions may endanger the imperfect solutions that have improved so many Cambodian lives.

"Humanitarian intervention" is a term that has come into vogue in early 2000. But the examples of Somalia and Sierra Leone show that no outside force can rebuild a society when it collapses internally. Cambodia is going through a fragile recovery. Only Cambodians can complete the job. Outsiders cannot.

WHEN WINSTON CHURCHILL CHOSE TO WORK with Stalin against their common enemy, England's survival was at stake, and all was excused. Thirty years later, the West refused to work with Pol Pot against the Vietnamese, because no vital Western interest could be invoked to justify or excuse a flexible relationship such as the one that Churchill had with Stalin. In Pol Pot's case the rule "Thou shalt not have any discourse with a genocidal ruler" was strictly applied, and Western condemnation of any direct contact with Pol Pot, or his minions in the Khmer Rouge, was total. The tragedy for the Cambodian people is that the West, in applying this rule when its *own* vital interests were not threatened, did not stop to ask whether the vital interests of the *Cambodians* were at stake, or whether their suffering could have been mitigated if the West had been willing to modify its rule as it had with Stalin.

These attitudes have caused considerable difficulties for Western policymakers (in both Western Europe and North America) when it comes to Cambodia. Their attempts to fashion pragmatic solutions for the Cambodian problem (pragmatic solutions that necessarily *include* the

Khmer Rouge) have been excoriated by their press and parliamentarians in favor of morally pure policies *excluding* the Khmer Rouge. Curiously, these moral pursuits would also have opposed any Western military involvement against the Khmer Rouge, especially any new American military intervention in Indochina, leading one to ask: if you cannot eliminate them and you do not include them, how would it be possible to have a peace agreement? Without a peace agreement, how can you end Cambodia's agony and ensure its future as an independent state?

Nguyen Co Thach

Someday historians enjoying the same access to Vietnamese archives as we do now to Soviet archives might be able to document that the Vietnamese leaders, especially Nguyen Co Thach, a brilliant tactician, were able to exploit these Western attitudes to the hilt. He certainly did so at the Paris Peace Conference in August 1989. It is questionable whether that conference could have ever succeeded, given the hard-line leaders still in power in Hanoi then. Nevertheless, Nguyen Co Thach chose a brilliant tactic to scuttle the conference, a tactic that the West found hard to challenge: he insisted that the conference declaration should denounce the policies and practices of the Khmer Rouge. Since the Khmer Rouge were present at the conference, such a reference ensured that the conference would fail, and Vietnam would remain in control of Cambodia.

Role of Western Public Opinion

This could well be a fascinating issue for future historians to study: Why did Western public opinion not realize that its moral campaign against the Khmer Rouge was being used to immoral ends by others? It is equally surprising that many in the West were prepared to accept the Vietnamese claim that they provided the bulwark against the return of the Khmer Rouge when it was the Vietnamese military intervention in Cambodia in the early 1970s that paved the way for Pol Pot to gain power in Phnom Penh. This can be documented. It was the North Vietnamese army that decimated Lon Nol's army and paved the way for the youthful and relatively inexperienced Khmer Rouge forces to take over Cambodia. The Vietnamese praised Pol Pot's rule right up until the moment that they invaded. When they removed Pol Pot from power, they installed former Khmer Rouge cadres in his place.

There is absolutely no doubt that both Pol Pot and the Khmer Rouge deserve all the ignominy heaped upon them. Someday they should be brought to justice. The Vietnamese did the Cambodian people a great favor by removing Pol Pot. All this is true. It is equally true that the sole Vietnamese motive for invading Cambodia was to fulfill a long-standing historical ambition to establish hegemony over Indochina. Through the 1980s many Cambodians agreed that Cambodia faced the threat of extinction as an independent nation. Hence, they reluctantly accepted Pol Pot's argument that without the Khmer Rouge the Cambodian nation that had almost disappeared in the face of Vietnamese expansionism in the nineteenth century might not survive the same threat in the twentieth. Pol Pot may have been adept at exploiting a deep-seated Cambodian fear for his own political purposes, but one reason he could do so is that many in the West, insensitive to Cambodian history, insisted that the West should merely recognize the Vietnamese-installed regime of Hun Sen. In the eyes of many Cambodians, acceptance of the Vietnamese occupation could have meant the extinction of the Cambodian nation. That was the fundamental reason why many worked with Pol Pot, directly or indirectly.

In short, what these Cambodians did in working with Pol Pot was what Churchill did in working with Stalin — work with a genocidal ruler for national survival. Yet all Cambodians who worked with Pol Pot were later vilified, including Prince Sihanouk (but not Hun Sen). Few stopped to consider whether these Cambodians had a legitimate fear that under the Vietnamese, Cambodia could disappear as a nation and the Cambodian people could end up like the Kurds. This is what happened to a minority group in Cambodia, the Chams, who had been driven into Cambodia and out of their homeland by Vietnamese expansionism in previous centuries. The Cambodians did not want to suffer the same fate.

From the viewpoint of the Cambodians, the ferocious Western crusade against Pol Pot and his Khmer Rouge had many paradoxical aspects. On the one hand it demonstrated the enormous Western concern over the fate of the Cambodians. Many of those who took part in these campaigns were well intentioned. However, in the great Western concern that the Khmer Rouge should be eliminated at all costs (but *without* any overt Western military involvement), they failed to see that this campaign was being exploited by those whom the Cambodians considered equally or more dangerous in the long run: the Vietnamese. The underlying attitude toward the Cambodians in many newspaper editorials was "we know that Hun Sen is imperfect, but as he is the best available, take him." It would have been fair for a Cambodian to respond: Would any Western society accept such potentially lethal colonization for themselves?

Unfortunately for the Cambodians, the Western attitude toward the Vietnamese was complicated by a peculiar problem in the American psyche, the hangover from the Vietnam War. Cambodia's age-old problem with Vietnamese expansionism in Indochina (an expansionism as natural as the United States' expansionism into Mexican territory) somehow became entangled with the efforts of many Americans to come to terms with their own involvement in Indochina, especially with their assessments of Vietnam.

This meant that questions asked by Cambodians were not asked in the West. For example, it would be reasonable for the Cambodians to ask whether they would have been better off if the anti–Vietnam War movement had failed. Would there have been no Pol Pot then? The record of those who remained silent in the Nazi holocaust has been well studied. But the record of those who encouraged the forces that led to Pol Pot's takeover in 1975 has not even been touched. It is still too sensitive.

If there had been no hangover from the Vietnam War — if some in the West had not been looking for ways to justify to themselves their support for North Vietnam, their country's enemy, during the war — would so many in the West have accepted so easily the Vietnamese argument that they had gone into Cambodia to save the Cambodian people from the Khmer Rouge? Looking dispassionately at the events of 1978–79 that led up to the Vietnamese invasion, it is clear that Cambodia was a pawn in a complex power struggle involving the

Soviet Union, China, and Vietnam. However, instead of focusing on the victim's plight in being caught once again in a power struggle of giants, much of the Western media focused on the Khmer Rouge issue, thereby tacitly condoning the Vietnamese invasion of Cambodia. The Cambodians found themselves in a bizarre situation: many in the West were trying to rescue them from yesterday's plight while the then ongoing power game involving Cambodia as a pawn continued unabated and underreported.

The UN Peace Agreement

It is something of a miracle that despite the public distortion of some of the key issues involved, a comprehensive peace agreement on Cambodia was reached in October 1991. In one of the greatest historical ironies of the twentieth century, all those who tried to use Cambodia as a pawn — the Soviet Union, China, and Vietnam — came to grief, and by late 1991, none wanted the troublesome task of maintaining their hold on Cambodia. The solution was an agreement that was both brilliant and simple. To "save face" (an Asian requirement) none of the key protagonists was acknowledged as the victor. In place of the two claimants to Cambodian leadership, a Supreme National Council was created to serve as the nominal legal repository of the country's sovereignty, but effective power was handed over to a UN administration that would run the country until UN-supervised elections could be held. A ceasefire took effect as soon as the agreement was signed. All the military forces in Cambodia would be regrouped and cantoned, and 70 percent of them eventually would be disarmed. External military supplies would cease. Most important, as the Cambodians would not vote for the Khmer Rouge (present or former cadres), free and impartial elections would effectively prevent the return to power of the Khmer Rouge. They would be consigned to the same fate as all the other Communist parties of the non-Communist states in Southeast Asia: spent forces, left to languish in the jungles.

The peace agreement was a wonderful development. Almost immediately after its signing a new chapter opened in Southeast Asian history, beginning a process of reconciliation among the long-divided

ASEAN and Indochinese states. Every state in the region supported it. Yet after its signing, the Cambodian people found themselves again a victim of Western contradictions.

Under the provisions of the agreement, two Khmer Rouge delegates returned to Phnom Penh in December 1991. Demonstrations were organized to protest their return. Violence flared out of control. One of the Khmer Rouge delegates, Khieu Samphan, was almost hanged. In their reporting and analysis of this event, almost all the Western media claimed that these were *spontaneous* demonstrations against the Khmer Rouge, failing to ask the obvious question: How could spontaneous demonstrations suddenly surface in a country so traumatized by war and repression? The editorials focused on how terrible it was that the Khmer Rouge were again being foisted on the Cambodian people. A *Washington Post* editorial (Sunday, 1 December 1991) said, for example, "Forgetting the past means forgetting the people who were murdered. That is precisely what the Cambodian people are unable and, to their credit, unwilling to do." These papers could not and did not report the real truth: forces in the Hun Sen regime were trying to scuttle the agreement, because they also feared the ballot box. The Khmer Rouge would have great difficulty winning UN-supervised elections, but so would the Hun Sen regime.

Fortunately, in this particular incident, the truth was to surface a few months later. The *New Yorker* carried an extensive description that revealed how the whole incident was stage-managed by the Hun Sen regime. The article said, "While Cambodians had every justification for rising up in anger and attacking the Khmer Rouge compound, the fact is that nothing in Cambodia happens spontaneously."[1] The day before Khieu Samphan's return students at the Phnom Penh University were given placards written by Hun Sen's Ministry of the Interior and told to go and demonstrate against the return of the Khmer Rouge. When the actual attacks on Khieu Samphan occurred, only twenty or thirty young men, speaking Cambodian with Vietnamese accents, were involved. They were far outnumbered by the policemen and soldiers present. Instead of restraining the attackers, the policemen helped them along. How could the dozens of Western reporters who were present in Phnom

Penh then get their story so wrong? Were they afraid that in reporting the truth they would do the Khmer Rouge a favor? How could they have failed to notice that the demonstrations would help those trying to scuttle the peace process, a point, as the *New Yorker* article points out, that was obvious to the Cambodian students? Only the *Economist* (7 December 1991, page 14) was brave enough to say that those who supported the peace agreement should defend the continued presence of the Khmer Rouge delegates in Phnom Penh until elections were held.

That dangerous moment passed. The Khmer Rouge delegates returned to Phnom Penh. The external forces that wanted peace in Cambodia prevailed on the Hun Sen regime to cease its mischief. The UN peace agreement is back on track. Yet it is more than likely that other such dangerous moments will arise until peace is finally restored to Cambodia.

Some American congressmen have threatened to withhold funding for the UN peace plan on the grounds that it confers "political and moral legitimacy upon the Khmer Rouge" and that it "relies too heavily upon Khmer Rouge cooperation for its success."[2] Their intention is to rescue the Cambodians from the Khmer Rouge. But if they succeed in cutting off the funding, the peace plan will disappear, war will resume, and the Khmer Rouge will be back in their element. Once again, if these congressmen succeed, the morally correct position will lead to disaster for the Cambodians. Elizabeth Becker has wisely reminded them that in 1975 it was the congressional decision to "cut back American aid to the Phnom Penh regime," on the grounds that it "would bring peace more swiftly to Cambodia," that led to the Khmer Rouge victory.[3] The Cambodians earnestly hope that Congress will not repeat the mistake it made in 1975.

Moral Outrage vs. Clinical Treatment

When a new disease or plague emerges, even out of human neglect or willfulness, any moral outrage against its emergence is normally accompanied by dispassionate and clinical analysis to find both its cause and cure. The Khmer Rouge represent no less than a plague on Cambodian society. The outrage has surfaced. The clinical analysis has not, creating yet another moral paradox. How can all those who spent so much time expressing outrage at the Khmer Rouge not devote equal time to finding effective solutions to stamp out the Khmer Rouge?

The Left, in both its old and new forms, fought the hardest against dispassionate analysis of the Khmer Rouge, accusing any poor soul who tried to do so of moral insensitivity. There was a reason for this virulence. The Left has a powerful vested interest in portraying the Khmer Rouge as a unique pathological phenomenon not linked to any other leftist movements. The truth, however, is that Pol Pot represents not a unique disease but only the most extreme form of a common one: the plague of communism. The fundamental mistake that Pol Pot and his colleagues made was to interpret Marx and Lenin literally. When these founders of the communist movement called for the extermination of the bourgeoisie, Pol Pot assumed that this meant physical elimination, not just their elimination as a political force. In their early years of power, Pol Pot and his colleagues took great pride that the purest form of communism in the world was to be found in Cambodia. Further dispassionate analysis of the origins of Pol Pot will also show that he could never have come to power on his own. He was propelled into Phnom Penh on the back of the Vietnamese revolution, which in turn received massive support from both the Soviet Union and China.

Such dispassionate analysis actually produces hope for the Cambodian people on at least four counts. First, if Pol Pot was swept into power in Phnom Penh with the high tide of communism, his chances of getting back into power are slim because this high tide has ebbed. Pol Pot and his movement survive like a few marine species stranded in a small pool left behind on the beach, far from the receded shoreline. If the tide does not come back to rescue them, they are doomed in a hostile environment. Southeast Asia represents such a hostile environment. It experienced many huge waves of communist expansionism, with communist parties running riot in virtually all Southeast Asian societies. Today the pathetic relics that remain in Thailand, Malaysia, and Indonesia survive only as spent forces. Eventually the Khmer Rouge will share the same fate. The tide of history is against them.

Second, the correlation of forces, to use a favorite Marxist expression, that propelled Pol Pot into Phnom Penh cannot be re-created.

Instead, the new correlation of forces favors their eventual extinction if only because all of their supporters in the 1970s (the Soviet Union, China, and Vietnam), each for their own reasons, want to see the effective implementation of the UN Cambodian peace agreement. This correlation of forces should be exploited by those implementing the UN peace agreement. If either the Khmer Rouge or the Hun Sen regime violate the peace agreement, their respective patrons should be held accountable for their behavior.

Third, if both Pol Pot and his offshoot, the Hun Sen regime, represent nothing more than versions of communist rule, their behavior can be *predicted*. Communism is not a new phenomenon. There is enough evidence available on the methods that communists use to gain power. Under Leninist rules all is justified in the fight for power. Lying and cheating are routine. Both the Khmer Rouge and the Hun Sen regime demonstrated this in the early days of the UN plan. The Khmer Rouge are violating the peace accords by denying the UN access to territories under their control. The Hun Sen regime (although it is divided) is violating the accords by unleashing its thugs to wipe out or intimidate Cambodians trying to form new political parties. The media reports have expressed surprise that this should be happening. A basic book on communist tactics should have told them what was going to happen. The UN should employ a few experienced anti-communist tacticians to help it anticipate the political actions of the Cambodian communists. Their mind-set is known; therefore, the behavior can be predicted.

Fourth, and finally, intelligent tactics should be used against the Khmer Rouge. If the Khmer Rouge believe that the UN plan will be rigged against them in the implementation process, they will only fight like cornered rats, giving no quarter, spilling even more blood. However, if they are convinced that the UN plan will be implemented fairly and impartially, they may give it a try. The Khmer Rouge leaders believe, contrary to Western perceptions, that they still enjoy political support, for at least two reasons. First, they believe that they represent the least corrupted force in Cambodia. Second, with their impressive anti-Vietnamese credentials, they can portray themselves as true nationalists, as they are trying to do.

Extending the analogy of the beached marine species, there is nothing that would kill these species faster than exposure to the open sun. Hence, they will make every effort to look for rocks under which to hide. In the case of the Khmer Rouge, the best tactic would be to lure them out from under the rocks and into the open political arena, where they and their supporters will face both the Cambodian population and the international community. They must be made to feel safe before they will emerge. The subdued response of the international community to the attempted lynching of Khieu Samphan sent the wrong message to the Khmer Rouge: that the international community would not protest strongly if other Cambodian parties violated the agreement. This will drive them farther away from the sunlight.

It will be emotionally difficult for some of the Western officials involved in the UN operations to be strictly impartial in dealing with the Khmer Rouge. The temptation to work against them, or to remain silent when the Phnom Penh regime attacks the Khmer Rouge, will be strong. But nothing could imperil the peace agreement more than the perception that it was not being fairly implemented. One should always bear in mind that the best poison pill that could be administered to the Khmer Rouge and guarantee their eventual disappearance from the Cambodian scene is the open, impartial, and effective implementation of the UN peace agreement. When all the Cambodian armed forces are disarmed and cantoned, and when the citizens of Phnom Penh feel that they can speak freely and not fear assassination, as they do now, by thugs sent out by the Phnom Penh regime, then a new political chemistry will emerge on the Cambodian scene. In this new political chemistry, Cambodian society will go along with the global trend and reject all forms of communism, whether of the Pol Pot or the Hun Sen variety. The anomalous situation today, where the strongest and best-financed Cambodian forces are the communist groups, will then end.

Conclusion

Through 1992 and 1993 the Cambodians will earnestly hope and pray that the imperiled UN peace plan will be successfully implemented and deliver them from two decades of agony. Their fate hangs on its successful implementation. If it fails, it will rob the Cambodians of what is effectively their last chance of deliverance from decades of suffering.

In these circumstances, there are a number of questions that the Cambodians could well ask. Why did the ferocious Western campaign against the Khmer Rouge, which elevated Pol Pot to the ranks of great historical villains such as Hitler and Stalin while he (Pol Pot) was still alive, have so little *practical* effect on the Cambodian people? Why did the Cambodian problem take so long to be solved even though it became one of the most powerful symbols of twentieth-century tragedy in the Western mind at a time when the West was globally dominant? Why did Western governments find it so difficult to pay for the UN peace operations when both their citizens and media were so exercised by the Cambodian tragedy? Even more curiously, at the precise historical moment when capitalism declared its victory over communism, the two best-financed Cambodian political forces remained the communist forces: the Khmer Rouge through their access to the Pailin diamond mines, and the Hun Sen regime through their ability to raise money in a corrupt fashion in Phnom Penh. Why did the two noncommunist forces have so much difficulty raising matching funds in the West? What was the moral value of championing causes *without* paying any heed to the consequences of these campaigns? This may not have been the first time that it has occurred. To quote once again from Max Weber's *Politics as a Vocation,* "If . . . one chases after the ultimate good in a war of beliefs, following a pure ethic of absolute ends, then the goals may be damaged and discredited for generations, because responsibility for *consequences* is lacking, and the diabolic forces which enter the play remain unknown to the actor."[4]

Perhaps the best response that the West can give to all these questions is to cease its efforts to find morally pure solutions for the Cambodian people and instead concentrate on ensuring that the UN peace plan is effectively and fully implemented. When that is done Cambodia could well be transformed from a symbol of tragedy to a symbol of hope in the twentieth century, and the Western conscience would be fully assuaged.

THE DANGERS OF DECADENCE: WHAT THE REST CAN TEACH THE WEST

In the summer of 1993 Samuel P. Huntington published "The Clash of Civilizations?" in Foreign Affairs. *A contradiction developed in the Western response to this essay: the intellectual establishment, by and large, denounced it, but the attention and debate it sparked suggested that Huntington had struck a resonant chord in Western minds. When* Foreign Affairs *asked me to contribute a response, I thought it would be worth explaining again that even though the West was now beginning to feel threatened by the Rest, in reality it was the Rest that had more reason to feel threatened by the West. If I had to rewrite the essay today, I would, with hindsight, remove some of its sharper edges.*

By the late 1990s, especially after the East Asian financial crisis, Huntington's thesis appeared to fade away. However, it had a dramatic resurgence after the tragic events of September 11, 2001. In the fifth paragraph of this essay, I had written: "Since the bombing of the World Trade Center, Americans have begun to absorb the European paranoia about Islam, perceived as a force of darkness hovering over a virtuous Christian civilization." These words were written not in 2001 but in the fall of 1993 after the attempted truck bombing of the World Trade Center.

As this book goes to press, in fall 2001, it is far too early to tell what lasting impact the events of September 11, 2001, will have. But clearly they will affect the fabric of the relationship between Western and Eastern, especially Islamic, societies. The need for cross-cultural understanding has never been greater.

It is also clear that if we want to prevent Huntington's thesis from becoming a reality — and this must surely be a universal, planetary wish

— we have to work harder to understand how to handle the potential causes of such a clash. Huntington is right in one respect: there will be great shifts of power. Our main challenge in the twenty-first century, as this essay argues, is to develop a long-term strategy to manage the shifts in the relative weight of civilizations.

IN KEY WESTERN CAPITALS there is a deep sense of unease about the future. The confidence that the West would remain a dominant force in the twenty-first century, as it has for the past four or five centuries, is giving way to a sense of foreboding. The emergence of fundamentalist Islam, the rise of East Asia, and the collapse of Russia and Eastern Europe could pose real threats to the West. A siege mentality is developing. Within these troubled walls Samuel P. Huntington's essay "The Clash of Civilizations?" is bound to resonate. It will, therefore, come as a great surprise to many Westerners to learn that the rest of the world fears the West even more than the West fears it, especially the threat posed by a wounded West.

Huntington is right: power is shifting among civilizations. But when the tectonic plates of world history move in a dramatic fashion, as they do now, perceptions of these changes depend on where one stands. The key purpose of this essay is to sensitize Western audiences to the perceptions of the rest of the world.

The retreat of the West is not universally welcomed. There is still no substitute for Western leadership, especially American leadership. Sudden withdrawals of American support from Middle Eastern or Pacific allies, albeit unlikely, could trigger massive changes that no one would relish. Western retreat could be as damaging as Western domination.

By any historical standard, the recent era of Western domination, especially under American leadership, has been remarkably benign. One dreads to think what the world would have looked like if either Nazi Germany or Stalinist Russia had triumphed in what have been called the "Western civil wars" of the twentieth century. Paradoxically, the benign nature of Western domination may be the source of many problems. Today most Western policymakers, who are children of their time, cannot conceive of the possibility that their own words and deeds could lead to evil, not good. The Western media aggravate this genuine blindness. Most Western journalists travel overseas with Western assumptions. They cannot understand how the West could be seen as anything but benevolent. CNN is not the solution. The same visual images transmitted simultaneously into living rooms across the globe can trigger opposing perceptions. Western living rooms applaud when cruise missiles strike Baghdad. Most living outside see that the West will deliver swift retribution to nonwhite Iraqis or Somalis but not to white Serbians, a dangerous signal by any standard.

The Asian Hordes

Huntington discusses the challenge posed by Islamic and Confucian civilizations. Since the bombing of the World Trade Center, Americans have begun to absorb European paranoia about Islam, perceived as a force of darkness hovering over a virtuous Christian civilization. It is ironic that the West should increasingly fear Islam when daily the Muslims are reminded of their own weakness. "Islam has bloody borders," Huntington says. But in all conflicts between Muslims and pro-Western forces, the Muslims are losing, and losing badly, whether they be Azeris, Palestinians, Iraqis, Iranians, or Bosnian Muslims. With so much disunity, the Islamic world is not about to coalesce into a single force.

Oddly, for all this paranoia, the West seems to be almost deliberately pursuing a course designed to anger the Islamic world. The West protests the reversal of democracy in Myanmar, Peru, and Nigeria, but not in Algeria. These double standards hurt. Bosnia has wreaked incalculable damage. The dramatic passivity of powerful European nations as genocide was committed on their doorstep has torn away the thin veil of moral authority that the West had spun around itself as a legacy of its recent benign era. Few can believe that the West would have remained equally passive if Muslim artillery shells had been raining down on Christian populations in Sarajevo or Srebrenica.

Western behavior toward China has been equally puzzling. In the 1970s the West developed a love affair with a China ruled by a regime that had committed gross atrocities during the Great Leap Forward and the Cultural Revolution. But when Mao Zedong's disastrous rule was followed by the far more benign Deng Xiaoping era, the West punished China for what, by its historical standards, was a minor crackdown: the Tiananmen incident.

Unfortunately Tiananmen has become a contemporary Western legend created by live telecasts of the crackdown. Beijing erred badly in its excessive use of firearms, but it did not err in its decision to crack down. Failure to quash the student rebellion could have led to political disintegration and chaos, a perennial Chinese nightmare. Western policymakers concede this in private. They are also aware of the dishonesty of some Western journalists: dining with student dissidents and even egging them on before reporting on their purported "hunger strike." No major Western journal has exposed this dishonesty or developed the political courage to say that China had virtually no choice in Tiananmen. Instead, sanctions were imposed, threatening China's modernization. Asians see that Western public opinion — deified in Western democracy — can produce irrational consequences. They watch with trepidation as Western policies on China lurch to and fro, threatening the otherwise smooth progress of East Asia.

Few in the West are aware that their governments and policymakers are responsible for aggravating turbulence among the more than two billion people living in Islamic and Chinese civilizations. Conjuring up images of the two Asian hordes that Western minds fear most — two forces that did, in the past, invade Europe, the Muslims and the Mongols — Huntington posits instead a Confucian-Islamic alliance against the West. American arms sales to Saudi Arabia do not suggest a natural Christian-Islamic connection. Neither should Chinese arms sales to Iran. Both are opportunistic moves based not on natural empathy or civilizational alliances. The real tragedy of suggesting a Confucian-Islamic connection is that it obscures the fundamentally different nature of the challenge posed by these forces. The Islamic world will have great difficulty modernizing. Until then its turbulence will spill over into the West. East Asia, including China, is poised to achieve parity with the West. The simple truth is that East and Southeast Asia feel more comfortable with the West.

This failure to develop a viable strategy to deal with Islam or China reveals a fatal flaw in the West: an inability to come to terms with the shifts in the relative weights of civilizations that Huntington convincingly documents. Two key sentences in his essay, when put side by side, illustrate the nature of the problem: first, "In the politics of civilizations, the peoples and governments of non-Western civilization no longer remain the objects of history as targets of Western colonization but join the West as movers and shapers of history," and second, "The West in effect is using international institutions, military power and economic resources to run the world in ways that will maintain Western predominance, protect Western interests and promote Western political and economic values." This combination is a prescription for disaster.

Simple arithmetic demonstrates Western folly. The West has 800 million people; the Rest make up almost 4.7 billion. In the national arena no Western society would accept a situation where 15 percent of its population legislated for the remaining 85 percent. But this is what the West is trying to do globally.

Tragically the West is turning its back on the Third World just when it can finally help the West out of its economic doldrums. The developing world's dollar output increased in 1992 more than that of North America, the European Community, and Japan put together. Two-thirds of the increase in U.S. exports has gone to the developing world. Instead of encouraging this global momentum by completing the Uruguay Round, the West is doing the opposite. It is trying to create barriers, not remove them. French Prime Minister Edouard Balladur tried to justify this move by saying bluntly in Washington that the "question now is how to organize to protect ourselves from countries whose different values enable them to undercut us."

The West's Own Undoing

Huntington fails to ask one obvious question: If other civilizations have been around for centuries, why are they posing a challenge only now? A sincere attempt to answer this question reveals a fatal flaw that has recently developed in the Western mind: an inability to conceive that the West may have developed structural weaknesses in its core value systems and institutions. This flaw explains, in part, the recent rush to embrace the theory that history has ended with the triumph of the Western ideal, the assumption being that individual freedom and democracy will always guarantee that Western civilization stays ahead of the pack.

Only hubris can explain why so many Western societies are trying to defy the economic laws of gravity. Budgetary discipline is disappearing. Expensive social programs and pork-barrel projects multiply with little heed to costs. The West's low savings and investment rates lead to declining competitiveness vis-à-vis East Asia. The work ethic is eroding while politicians delude workers into believing that they can retain high wages despite becoming internationally uncompetitive. Leadership is lacking. Any politician who states hard truths is immediately voted out. Americans freely admit that many of their economic problems arise from the inherent gridlock of American democracy. While the rest of the world is puzzled by these fiscal follies, American politicians and journalists travel around the world preaching the virtues of democracy. It makes for a curious sight.

The same hero-worship is given to the idea of individual freedom. Much good has come from this idea. Slavery ended. Universal franchise followed. But freedom does not only solve problems; it can also cause them. The United States has undertaken a massive social experiment, tearing down social institution after social institution that restrained the individual. The results have been disastrous. Since 1960 the U.S. population has increased 41 percent while violent crime has risen by 560 percent, single-mother births by 419 percent, divorce rates by 300 percent, and children living in single-parent homes by 300 percent. This is massive social decay. Many a society shudders at the prospect of this happening on its shores. But instead of traveling overseas with humility, Americans confidently preach the virtues of unfettered individual freedom, blithely ignoring the visible social consequences.

The West is still the repository of the greatest assets and achievements of human civilization. Many Western values explain the spectacular advance of mankind: the belief in scientific inquiry, the search for rational solutions, and the willingness to challenge assumptions. But a society that believes it is practicing these values can be led to a unique blindness: it cannot see that some of the values that come with the package may be harmful. Western values do not form a seamless web. Some are good. Some are bad. But one has to stand outside the West to see this clearly and to see how the West's relative decline is being brought about by its own hand. Huntington, too, is blind to this.

THE REST OF THE WEST?

*In the summer of 2000 I was invited by BBC World Radio and the Royal
Society of Arts to deliver one of the four BBC World Lectures for the year in
London. I felt flattered. BBC World Radio has a global audience of millions.
I hoped my lecture would reach most of them. Fortunately the BBC was
wiser. Lectures don't travel well over radio. Instead the BBC interviewed me.
This lecture was posted on the Web site and is reprinted here for the first time.*

*This essay brings to an end not just this section of the volume but also a
phase of my writing career. It completes the thought processes initiated in
"The West and the Rest." Much of our global history has been written from
the perspective of Western intellectuals. This essay documents this point.
And it also makes the case that this five-hundred-year cycle of Western
domination of the world is coming to an end.*

*One key point is worth stressing in this introductory note. In an effort
to create a level playing field for the contest of ideas between Eastern and
Western civilizations, I have had to naturally speak more critically of the
West, because at present the field — in the media, academia, and
publishing universes — is badly skewed against non-Western perspectives.
But I have never been anti-Western. Indeed, as one of my Western friends
recently reminded me, my essay "The West and the Rest" actually provides
sterling praise of the qualities that lifted Western societies to new heights.*

*The conclusion of this essay may therefore surprise those readers who
may have believed that I had an anti-Western bias. Western domination
may end, but Western civilization will continue to remain a vibrant and
dynamic force for centuries to come. But as it does so it will not remain the*

same. The West too will be inevitably transformed and, as I say in the last paragraph, transformed in a way that my friends in the West should view as an optimistic conclusion.

LET ME BEGIN WITH TWO ARAB PROVERBS. One says, "The man who speaks about the future lies, even when he tells the truth." Another says, "For every glance behind us, we have to look twice to the future." These two Arab proverbs capture well the challenge I face in this lecture. I am going to address the future, not the past, and all discussions of the future are inherently perilous.

My thesis is a relatively simple one: that the twenty-first century will be fundamentally different from the nineteenth and twentieth centuries. By the end of the century, we will return — in terms of balance of civilizations — to the world we saw somewhere between A.D. 1000 and 1500. I don't know exactly when these great changes will manifest themselves clearly. I hope that they will emerge clearly in the next twenty-five years, while I have a chance to be around to witness them. But even if they do not happen in the next decade or two, I remain confident that great change will occur this century. I feel this deeply in my bones.

My underlying premise is that the West has played an unusually dominant role in world history for the past two centuries or more. Many history books have made this point. One such classic is *The Rise of the West* by William H. McNeill.[1] Another historian, J. M. Roberts, has this to say in his *Triumph of the West.*

> It seems reasonable to expect agreement that the course of "modern" history . . . has been increasingly dominated by first the Europeans and then the Western civilization which was its successor. By "dominated" I mean two things were going on. One was that the history of the rest of the globe was changed forever and irreversibly by the actions of the men of the West. The other was that it changed in a particular direction; it was overwhelmingly a matter of other cultures taking up Western ideas, goals and values, not the reverse.[2]

So, to summarize world history crudely, for most of the past two hundred years Western populations have been subjects of world history while the rest of the world have been objects.

As a consequence of dominating the world for two centuries or more, the West has spun several layers of influence around the globe, which in one way or another perpetuate that domination. Curiously, most Western minds cannot see the layers of Western influence, because they have spent most of their lives above these layers. Those who live under them know how extensive and deep they are — and those who, like me, have traveled from beneath the layers to climb over them can perhaps see both sides of the picture. And only this transition that I have made in my life has emboldened me to make the outrageous claims that I will make here.

A small personal anecdote may help explain what life was like under the layers. Forty-six years ago, when I went to school for the first time in Singapore, then a British colony, I once asked my classmate Morgan where he wanted to be when he grew up. He replied, "London, of course." I asked why. He replied, "Because in London the streets are paved with gold." This was how mighty and strong London appeared to be in our young minds. British colonial rule has long gone, but that removed only one layer of Western influence. Other layers remain.

The main conclusion I wish to draw is that sometime in the twenty-first century we will see what I will call the Rest of the West. There is a deliberate "double entendre" in my use of the word "Rest": to connote both passivity and remainder.

Having said that my subject will be the rest of the West, let me quickly add that I do not belong to the Western school of declinists. I do not foresee the decline and fall of Western civilization. Indeed, the West will remain dynamic and active for most of the twenty-first century, and it may well remain the primary civilization for a long time more. But what is likely to end is its domination of the world. I see this as neither a happy nor a sad conclusion. I have argued many times previously that for the past few centuries the West has borne the primary burden of advancing human civilization. The huge leaps in science and technology have resulted in huge increases in the standard and quality of life for much of mankind, as well as the significant new ideas in social and political philosophy that have generated revolutionary ideas of freedom and equality for all men, have all emerged from Western societies. Mankind today would have been in a sorry state if the West had not transformed itself into the most dynamic civilization on earth. But since it has carried the burden of advancing mankind's fortunes for several centuries, perhaps it is time that we gave the West a rest.

At the same time I would like to send a message of hope to the five-sixths of the world's population who live outside the West. If my thesis is proven correct then the two centuries during which they have essentially been passengers on the bus will end. In this coming century, if they learn the lessons of history well, they may finally get the opportunity to be codrivers of the global bus. And, to be honest, my reason for choosing this topic was precisely to send out this message of hope. Most living in the West do not appreciate or understand the feeling among many in the Third World that they are essentially second-class citizens of our globe. They need to believe that they too can become first-class citizens.

One key lesson of history is that change has never been easy or smooth. Often it has been difficult or turbulent. To capture some of the difficulties of the process of change, I am going to borrow the Hegelian/Marxist dialectical concept of change — that change takes place in a process of thesis, antithesis, and synthesis. My thesis will be that even today the world continues to be dominated by the West. My antithesis will be about the forces bringing about the end of Western domination, and my synthesis will be about the Rest of the West. The image I mentioned, of a world still covered by layers of Western influence, will describe my thesis. My antithesis will describe how these layers will retreat from the globe, and my synthesis will, I hope, give a glimpse of the world to come when these layers retreat.

The Thesis

In the post-colonial era, any thesis of continual Western domination does appear to be counterintuitive. With the advent of the UN Charter, all nation-states can claim to enjoy sovereign equality. This is the theory. In reality, nation-states — like human beings in any society — do not enjoy equal power. What is remarkable is that today, in many significant ways, the architecture of power relationships in the beginning of the twenty-first century still resembles those of the nineteenth century.

Let me add a quick qualification. The means of using or exercising this power has changed significantly. With the disappearance of the colonial era, and especially after the end of World War II, we have not often seen the brutal use of military force to invade and occupy neighboring countries, with rare exceptions such as the invasions of Afghanistan and Cambodia a decade or so ago. But real power can be exercised in many different forms. And if one looks beneath the surface it is remarkable how little things have changed since the nineteenth century.

This brief essay does not allow me to provide an encyclopedic portrayal of power relationships around the world. But a few examples may help to illustrate my thesis. And I will move from examples of "hard" power to examples of "soft" power (to borrow a phrase created by Joseph Nye of Harvard University) and illustrate the continuing inequalities in the world.

First, let us look at the military dimension. In the nineteenth century Western military power could not be challenged. Today this continues to be so. The North Atlantic Treaty Organization (NATO) remains the single most powerful military organization in the world. Four out of the five (including Russia) official nuclear powers are Western. Only the United States has the ability to project its military power anywhere in the world. No non-Western power can dream of doing this. It is true that such military power is rarely used today. But, if required, it can be used. The citizens of Belgrade and Baghdad understand this well.

In the economic sphere one could also argue that there have been no fundamental changes in the architecture of economic power. The relative share of the global gross national product (GNP) of the United States and Western (and now Eastern) Europe remain about the same as in the nineteenth century. Accurate statistics are hard to come by. But it is clear that today the Group of Seven (G-7) countries (which include

Japan, both an Asian and a "Western" power) dominate global economic decisions. Most of the world's research and development is still being done in the countries of the OECD (which remains essentially a Western club). Equally important, the most important multilateral economic agencies — the IMF, the World Bank, the Bank for International Settlements (BIS), the WTO, the Financial Stability Forum — are dominated by the Western states. No non-Western citizen, not even a Japanese, has a realistic prospect of heading the IMF or World Bank.

As we move into the political sphere we move from the realm of "hard" power to "soft" power, partly because the exercise of political power has become more subtle. In the nineteenth century, during the colonial era, most of the countries of the world were mere pawns on a chessboard, while the players were European. In the twenty-first century all the countries of the United Nations are nominally equal. This nominal equality should not be dismissed. It has enhanced the sense of self-worth and dignity of many people around the world. But when it comes to making hard decisions on how and when the world's resources will be deployed, we should be under no illusion that all capitals are equal. Just as in the nineteenth century, a handful of capitals make the big decisions. Today the key capitals are Washington D.C., Berlin, Paris, Moscow, London, and gradually Tokyo and Beijing. The nineteenth-century list may not have been very different. And where the decisions are made makes a huge difference in the deployment of real resources. The minister of state for foreign affairs of Uganda, Amama Mbabazi, captured this reality vividly with this statement: "When it is Kosovo, you are there in one minute and spend billions. When it's East Timor you are there. When it is Africa, there are all sorts of excuses."[3] His statement accurately captures the consequence of unequal political power.

As I speak of the continuation of old forms of power, I know that some of you must be puzzled. Hasn't the world changed dramatically since the nineteenth century? Yes, it has. But the counterintuitive point I want to make is this: despite these important changes, the underlying architecture of power relationships has not changed significantly, either in the hard military and economic dimensions or the new soft dimensions of cultural and intellectual power.

Look, for example, at the fields of information and information technology: two key dimensions of our world today. Those who control the flow of information determine what content enters into billions of minds who have access to radios, TVs, and the Internet. Today all the sources of information with a global reach — whether it be CNN or BBC, the *Wall Street Journal* or *Financial Times, Time* magazine or the *Economist* — are all Western controlled. And it is Western minds who determine what news is significant and worth airing globally and what is not. This makes a crucial difference. To cite a simple example, if an Asian or African or Latin American princess were to pass away tomorrow, it would hardly be mentioned in the news. But when Princess Diana died it became a global event, because those who control global information flows decided that this was a global event. Let me stress that I am not passing judgment whether this is right or wrong. I am only trying to analyze realities dispassionately.

The West also dominates in many other areas: in universities, in research and development, in Nobel prizes for science, in the release of new technology. Virtually all the cutting-edge work in any field of science, perhaps even in social sciences, is done in the West. Equally important, in discussions of philosophy and human values, the greatest outpouring of writing and books is generated in the West. Hence, while we are not surprised that the United States should be passing moral judgment on the implementation of human rights instruments by China, a visitor from Mars might be surprised that a young two-hundred-year-old society of the world is passing judgment on a five-thousand-year-old society. In short, we take for granted a certain imbalance of power relationships as a normal and perhaps eternal feature of the human landscape. And this brings me to the second part of my argument: what we take to be normal and eternal may be changing. The antithesis is surfacing. The world is changing dramatically.

The Antithesis
One of the key insights Marx left with us is that economic change drives the world. And if he were alive today he would be amazed by the scope and speed of economic change we are witnessing. He would also

be puzzled by the conventional wisdom that these rapid economic changes will not lead to historic shifts in the political, ideological, or cultural landscapes of the world. When I showed a draft of this essay to my friends, they challenged my assertion that conventional wisdom in the West today states that nothing fundamental will change. So, to prove my point, let me cite two examples. In May 2000 the *Financial Times* carried a column by Michael Prowse in which he wrote, "I see the twenty-first century as belonging to Europe."[4] Another well-known writer, Robert Kaplan, used even more vivid imagery to describe the continuing Western domination. He compared the world in the twenty-first century to a "stretch limo in the potholed streets of New York City, where homeless beggars live." Inside the limo "are the air-conditioned post-industrial regions of North America, Europe, the emerging Pacific Rim" [Yes — this is a concession to a few outside the West]. Outside the limo "is the rest of mankind, going in a completely different direction." My vision of the future is sharply different from the perspectives of these two Western writers.

The main engine of change in the twenty-first century will be the forces of globalization. We are all aware that there is a raging debate going on about the virtue and vices of globalization. The demonstrators at the Seattle WTO and the Washington IMF meetings were trying to generate a consensus that globalization is bad. A column in the *New York Times* by Joseph Kahn in May 2000 seems to support this view with the observation that "among both mainstream economists and their left-leaning critics, it has become axiomatic that globalization leaves too many poor people behind."[5] Personally, I agree with the view that the UN secretary-general, Kofi Annan, recently expressed: "The cure does not lie in protesting against globalization itself. I believe the poor are poor not because of too much globalization, but because of too little — because they are excluded."[6]

Fortunately for us this debate is irrelevant. Globalization is an irreversible force. It has been unleashed by rapid technological change. We cannot turn the clock back. As a result of rapid technological change in many dimensions, the earth has shrunk. We have gone from being Planet Earth to Spaceship Earth. All of mankind has begun to be spun together in a complex web of interdependence. The consequences for our future are enormous.

The first consequence of interdependence is that we have a common stake in each other's economic well-being. The Asian financial crisis demonstrated this vividly. When the Thai baht collapsed on 2 July 1997, the major economic capitals paid little attention. The big global economic decision makers of that time decided that this little crisis on the other side of globe could be ignored.

But the crisis spread to other countries in Southeast Asia. From there it shook Korea. This in turn affected Russia. From Russia it leaped to Brazil and then, in an important leap, it began to rattle American markets. This episode demonstrates vividly how interdependent the world has become. The flow of currency around the world — U.S. $1.5 trillion a day — has become so large that no one can control it. With the global integration of all economies into one system, the strong economies now have to worry about the weaker economies, because, as Claude Smadja has observed: "In an increasingly integrated world, the resilience of the global economy is only as strong as the weakest of its components."[7] Another vivid example of global interdependence was demonstrated by the rapid spread of the "I love you" virus in a matter of days from a single computer in the Philippines to the whole world.

The positive effects of globalization should not be ignored. It provides a new economic tide, which has already integrated millions in the Third World into the modern world, especially in the two most populous nations, India and China. Although there remain huge numbers of poor people in India and China, globalization has already had spectacular effects in the social and economic landscapes of both countries. The economic successes of China are well known. Few are aware that India too is experiencing explosive economic growth. The recent UN Millennium Summit report predicted that by 2008 the Indian computer industry would reach $85 billion, a spectacular sum by any standard. Since the mid-1980s, when the economic success of Japan and the Four Tigers (Korea, Taiwan, Hong Kong, and Singapore) became evident, it was clear that their success would soon spread to other Asian societies. The Asian financial crisis of 1997–98 was a major hiccup, but it has not altered the upward economic trend. In the economic sphere Western domination will gradually decrease, and a more level playing field will emerge.

The interdependence I have spoken about in the economic field is also becoming apparent in the environmental field. Chernobyl taught us a valuable lesson: environmental disasters don't respect borders. Neither do new infectious diseases, which can be transported from one corner of the world to the other overnight. All Western populations, like the rest of the world, have an economic stake in the level of emissions that China and India produce as they industrialize and progress. I am not an expert in this field but if their per capita emissions reach half of the American level, the global environment will be seriously destabilized.

So far I have only illustrated interdependence in the economic and environmental fields. But it will logically and inevitably spread. And as interdependence grows, a crucial change will take place in the relationship between the West and the Rest: they will have to cooperate if they are to live together harmoniously on a shrinking planet. Interdependence reduces the capacity of one to dominate the other and creates a more level playing field between the two. For this reason, if for no other, the Third World should welcome the acceleration of globalization.

But growing interdependence and changing economic realities will not be the only forces reducing Western domination. Changing demographic relationships will have an equally profound effect. In previous centuries Western populations appeared to increase at the same pace as the rest of the world. For example, in the nineteenth century, when Britain dominated the world in many ways, its population almost quadrupled from about 10 million in 1801 to 37 million in 1901. In the twentieth century it did not quite double, rising only to about 60 million. In the twenty-first century the population of the UK, like that of most other European nations, is likely to remain stagnant.

This has created spectacular demographic disparities. The developed world's share of the global population will shrink from 24 percent in 1950 to 10 percent in 2050. In 1950 six of the twelve most populous nations in the world were Western. By 2050 there will be one: the United States. In 1950 Africa's population was less than half of Europe's (including Russia's). Today it is roughly the same. By 2050 Africa's population will be three times larger than Europe's.[8] It is hard to believe that such huge demographic shifts will have no serious social and political consequences.

Partly as a result of these demographic changes, partly as a result of economic and technological needs for new brainpower, partly as a result of TV images now informing the world's poor that a better life is attainable, there have been increasing flows of non-Western immigrants into Western societies. The most spectacular and successful example of this is in Silicon Valley; one reason for the Valley's success is said to be the IC factor. "IC" refers not to "Integrated Circuits" but to Indian and Chinese. Huge numbers of Indians and Chinese have provided the brainpower needed for new software and hardware developments. Incidentally, I should mention here that while the economic benefits from their brainpower may flow mainly into California, their spectacular performance significantly increases the cultural confidence as well as self-esteem of their native countries.

The United States, however, is accustomed to receiving new flows of immigrants. Europe is not. But in the twenty-first century this will change. The *Economist* (6–12 May 2000) carried a lengthy article on immigration into Europe. Because their populations are both aging and declining, most European nations will need more immigrants. Let me again quote the *Economist*: "To keep the ratio of workers to pensioners steady, the flow would need to swell to 3.6 million a year in Germany, 1.8 million a year in France and a staggering 13.5 million a year in the EU as a whole."[9]

The Meaning of this Antithesis
At this stage, the emphasis I am putting on demographic trends may be puzzling. But let me remind you of my initial image, of the globe surrounded by Western layers of influence. Let us consider how these layers began. First, what did the world look like at the beginning of the nineteenth century? Here I will again quote William H. McNeill from *The Rise of the West:*

At the outbreak of the French Revolution in 1789, the geographical boundaries of Western civilization could still be defined with reasonable precision (i.e. within Europe) . . . (But) within a few decades settlers of European origin or descent were able to occupy central and western North America, the pampas and adjacent regions of South America, and substantial parts of Australia, New Zealand, and South Africa.[10]

These population movements have had an enormous impact on nature and the character of civilizations. In *The Triumph of the West* J. M. Roberts notes that for most of the past five thousand years there have been several distinct civilizations living side by side, in the same world — but apart. He also adds:

Even when in direct geographical contact, or locked in open conflict, they seem always to have been separated by invisible membranes which, though permeable enough to permit some cross fertilisation, have proved immensely tough and enduring. Civilisations have co-existed for centuries, even sharing land frontiers, but still passing little to one another which led to any essential change in either. Their own unique natures remained intact.[11]

At this point, imagine the world preceding Western expansion to be one where different civilizations survived unaffected by other civilizations, like distinct and intact billiard balls. J. M. Roberts opens his book with this world as his starting point and then describes in great detail how all the civilizations of the world have been changed, transformed, affected by the explosion of Western civilizations over the past two centuries.

The process of change that he describes was a one-way street: the impact of the West upon the Rest (these are my words, not his). Indeed, in his concluding chapter, entitled "A Post-Western World," he speculates on how the world will turn out with the end of the Western expansionary phase. But he remains confident that Western civilization will provide the standard by which all other civilizations or societies will measure themselves. As he states:

Here lies the deepest irony of post-Western history: it is so often in the name of Western values that the West is rejected and it is always with its skills and tools that its grasp is shaken off. Western values and assumptions have been internalized to a remarkable degree in almost every other major culture.[12]

Indeed, his implicit assumption that Western civilization represents the apex of human civilization is a deeply held belief in Western minds. And this belief has also entered non-Western minds. V. S. Naipaul demonstrated this with his claim that Western civilization represents the only universal civilization.

The Synthesis

My conclusion is a remarkably simple one. Historians such as William McNeill and J. M. Roberts are correct in describing the central flow of history for the past two hundred years as a one-way street. McNeill writes:

But the West's expansion helped to precipitate a decisive break-through of older styles of civilized life in Asia about the middle of the nineteenth century. For a full hundred years thereafter, the non-Western world struggled to adjust local cultural inheritances in all their variety and richness to ideas and techniques originating in the European nineteenth century.[13]

I agree that this is how world history has flowed for the past two centuries. It has been a one-way street.

My prediction for the twenty-first century is an equally simple one: for the first time in centuries we will have a two-way street in the flow of ideas, values, and people. This notion of a two-way street of ideas is something very difficult for many Western intellectuals to conceive, because many believe that they have created the world in their own image. Please allow me to quote J. M. Roberts one more time: "Paradoxically, we may now be entering the era of its greatest triumph, not over state structures and economic relationships, but over the minds and hearts of all men. Perhaps they are Westerners now."[14]

The simple reality that J. M. Roberts did not grasp — and I must stress that in his book Roberts comes across as a wise and modest man, not as arrogant or close-minded — is that while Western ideas and best practices have found their way into the minds of all men, the hearts and souls of other civilizations remain intact. There are deep reservoirs of spiritual and cultural strength that have not been affected by the Western veneer that has been spread over many other societies. I began by referring to the layers that the West has spun around the globe. As we move into the twenty-first century, the retreat of these layers will reveal rich new human landscapes.

Only someone who has lived outside the West, as I have, can see both how powerful the impact of the West has been upon the rest of the world and at the same time how limited its impact has been on the souls of other peoples. The real paradox, contrary to J. M. Roberts, is not that Western culture has taken over the hearts and minds of all men but that Western ideas and technology will over time enable other societies to accumulate enough affluence and luxury to rediscover their own cultural roots.

Initially, when Asian populations acquired TV sets they watched Western dramas out of Hollywood. Many still do. But just as many Americans found the program *Roots* riveting, as it described a past they were only vaguely aware of, other non-Western societies have returned to their own roots, from which they had been effectively cut off for centuries. So in Asia, for example, each Asian society is beginning to reconnect with its past. Many in the West have heard in passing about the Hindu epics of Ramayana and Mahabharata. These epics have been absorbed heart and soul by young Indians with their mothers' milk. But most of the time it has been handed down orally or in print. When these epics were finally converted into TV dramas, hundred of millions of Indians stopped whatever they were doing to watch the re-creation of their cultural legacy through Western TV boxes. The same is happening or will happen in other Asian societies. All this will, to put it simply again, generate a renaissance of Asian cultures not seen in centuries.

I know that I am providing only a few examples of a changed world. Colleagues have complained to me that they can't imagine fully the world I was trying to predict. Neither can I. But let me suggest one area where we can look for leading indicators of the new world to come: the Internet universe. Today, I am told, 90 percent of the Web sites are in English. But the content of the Internet is driven not just by the producers but also by the consumers. If my predictions are right, the proportion of English Web sites will fall steadily and be replaced by a huge variety of languages. Let me add that there is one key structural reason why I have chosen the Internet as a leading indicator. Unlike Hollywood films, Western TV dramas, or CNN and BBC reportage of the world, all of which enter the eyes and minds of the rest of the world in a one-way flow, The Internet is unique in generating a two-way flow. And if my thesis of a coming two-way street of ideas and values is correct, the first evidence of this may also surface in the Internet universe.

All these great changes do not mean that all the Western layers that now envelop the world will disappear. J. M. Roberts is correct in saying that many Western ideas have proven to be utilitarian for both Western and non-Western societies. Good technology is race blind and color blind. It works for all. Medical advances in the West have benefited all mankind. So too will many Western social and political concepts. For example, if the rule of law (rather than rule by law) becomes entrenched in Asian societies, it may well be the crucial variable that enables them to lift themselves from their feudal practices. If meritocracy, rather than nepotism, became the norm of Asian societies, it would mean a tremendous unleashing of the brainpower found there. The real challenge non-Western societies will face in the twenty-first century will be in deciding which Western layers to retain and which to peel away.

The end of the era of Western domination will therefore not be a smooth or easy one for non-Western societies. If they reject all the Western legacy left in their societies they may throw the baby out with the bathwater. Each non-Western society, whether it be China, India, Indonesia, or Iran, will have to decide carefully which aspects of Western systems and culture can be retained and absorbed in their societies and which cannot. There is a monumental struggle going on within the souls of many Asians to decide what kind of identity they want for their future.

They are trying to find the best from their own cultural roots and the best from the West. This struggle is another reason why the next chapter of history is going to be an exciting one for the world.

At the same time the success of Silicon Valley shows that there is a natural "fit" between the brain food (now generated in the West) and the deep wealth of Asian brainpower (which remains untapped). Economic forces — unless interrupted by political or military disasters — will draw Western technology, capital, and exports closer to Asian workers and markets. If trade flows across the Pacific begin to grow faster than transatlantic flows, the U.S. links with Asia will deepen once more.

All this could lead to another significant new development in world history. Geography, some say, is destiny. Hitherto, the common historical and cultural roots of the United States and Europe have kept them close together despite the vast Atlantic Ocean that separates them. But over time their geographic, economic, and political needs could pull them in different directions. It is conceivable that the United States and Europe will march to a different drumbeat in the next century. So far all the trade and economic disputes between the United States and Europe have been resolved harmoniously. But if strains emerge, we should not be surprised.

All this brings me to my final paradoxical conclusion. Writers such as William McNeill and J. M. Roberts, who have documented the brilliant and magnificent contributions of the West for the past two centuries, share a deep conviction that the West will remain dynamic and vibrant. But as part of this continuing dynamism the West will increasingly absorb good minds from other cultures. And, as it does so, the West itself will undergo a transformation: it will become, within itself, a microcosm of the new interdependent world, containing many thriving cultures and ideas. The West may finally live up to its highest ideals and become a truly cosmopolitan society.

Again, when I speak about such a cosmopolitan destiny for the West, my friends frown and state that they cannot visualize it. Fortunately for me, the June 2000 issue of *National Geographic* has a wonderful article on London. London, it says, may well have become the most cosmopolitan city in the world. As the article said:

The whole world lives in London. Walk down Oxford Street and you will see Indians and Colombians, Bangladeshis and Ethiopians, Pakistanis and Russians, Melanesians and Malaysians. Fifty nationalities with communities of more than 5,000 make their home in the city, and on any given day 300 languages are spoken. It is estimated that by 2010 the population will be almost 30 percent ethnic minorities, the majority born in the U.K.[15]

I began this article by describing the central role London played in the former phase of Western history, when its streets appeared to be paved with gold. The transformation of London into a truly cosmopolitan city may indeed be a harbinger of things to come, not only for the U.K. but perhaps for most of the Western world.

The Rest of the West may therefore see the creation of a new civilization, which will truly integrate the best from all streams of mankind. I hope that my friends in the West will see this as an optimistic conclusion.

THE ASIA-PACIFIC

JAPAN ADRIFT

When I took a sabbatical at the Center for International Affairs in Harvard University in 1991–92, I was required to write a thesis on any subject of my choice. I chose to write on Japan, a country that had always fascinated me. In the fall of 1992 I wrote this essay for Foreign Policy *magazine as an extension of my research at the Center.*

Japan must surely be unique in the world. It was the first non-Western society to modernize, and the first to be admitted into exclusive Western clubs such as the G-7 and OECD. It has also been one of the most admired countries in Asia for its enormous economic achievements as well as for its social and spiritual stability.

Yet it may also be one of the loneliest countries in the world. When the Cold War ended and the Berlin Wall fell, James Baker, then U.S. secretary of state, announced that a new Western community would be created "from Vancouver to Vladivostok." The only major country left out of this magic circle was Japan, even though it had been the key ally of the United States in Northeast Asia. As a result it has had to find a new role and identity for itself in the post–Cold War era. The search goes on. Japan has still not found any natural resting place for itself. And yet it has had difficulties joining any East Asian community, as shown in the discomfort it experienced with Dr. Mahathir's idea of an East Asian Economic Grouping.

This paradox of being a member and at the same time a nonmember of key groupings is uniquely Japanese. Personally, I remain a great admirer of Japanese society. But the more I study it, the less I feel that I know it. Looking back, I am amazed by my audacity in publishing an essay on Japan when I am obviously no expert. Yet the central insight of the essay — that Japan has yet to find a natural resting place in the community of

*nations — continues to be valid. And there may not be a solution to this
Japanese condition in the near future. Japan may be adrift for a while.*

A JAPANESE FOLKTALE tells of a young boy who lives in a coastal
rice-farming village. One autumn morning, walking alone to work in
the fields, he sees, to his horror, an approaching tsunami, which he
knows will destroy the village. Knowing that he has no time to run
down the hill to warn the villagers, he sets the rice fields on fire, sure
that the desire to save their crops will draw all the villagers up the hill.
The precious rice fields are sacrificed, but the villagers are saved from
the tsunami. In what follows, some of the precious rice fields of strategic discourse in East Asia may burn, but in the process I hope to alert
readers to the wave of change that is approaching the region.

Most believe that Japan emerged from the Cold War a winner. As
former Senator Paul Tsongas put it during his presidential campaign:
"The Cold War is over and the Japanese won." The bursting of the
Japanese financial bubble in mid-1992 has somewhat undercut the
power of that claim, but no one suggests that the Cold War's end has
hurt Japan. Yet, in reality, Japan leaves the Cold War era more troubled
than satisfied, more threatened than secure.

Japanese strategic planners can point to many gains at the end of
the Cold War. The Soviet threat has all but disappeared. The chances of
a major war either close to or involving Japan seem extremely low.
China, which once overshadowed Japan, has since diminished in
stature, especially after the June 1989 massacre at Tiananmen Square.
The East Asian region, Japan's economic backyard, continues to prosper, boosted now by the economic takeoff of China's coastal provinces.
Japan has emerged as the world's second largest economic power, with
the prospect of overtaking the first, the United States, in a decade or
two. Even in absolute terms Japan already invests more for the future
than does the larger United States.

Despite those significant gains, Japan now faces its most difficult, if
not precarious, strategic environment since World War II. The Soviet
threat that drew Japan comfortably into the Western camp and provided the glue for the U.S.-Japanese security relationship is now gone.

Neither the United States nor Japan, each for its own reasons, is yet prepared to abandon the Mutual Security Treaty (MST). But the strategic pillars upon which the MST rested have eroded, leaving the Japanese to wonder whether — and under what circumstances — the United States will be willing to come to Japan's defense in the future.

The notion of a strategically insecure economic superpower is hard to swallow, but consider this: During the Cold War, Japanese security planners did not even consider the possibility of a rupture in the U.S.-Japanese security relationship. Now they do. If that tie breaks, Japan could find itself strategically vulnerable in the face of at least three potentially unfriendly, if not adversarial, neighbors: China, Korea, and Russia. To be sure, no military conflicts are imminent between Japan and any one of them. No war planning is required. But whereas Japan and its neighbors did not worry about each other during the Cold War, now they do. A *Beijing Review* article in February 1992 warned, "Japan has become more active and independent in conducting its foreign policy in an attempt to fill the vacancy in the Asia-Pacific region left by the withdrawal of US and Russian influences." And South Korean planners say that even after reunification, U.S. forces should stay in Korea to protect Korea from Japan.

The root cause of Japan's problems in the post–Cold War era is the troubled U.S.-Japanese relationship. The key security interests that held the two countries together — especially the containment of the Soviet Union — have diminished or disappeared. It is astonishing how that simple point is either missed or ignored in the analysis of Japanese foreign policy. Consider, for example, how much U.S. and Japanese interests have diverged over Russia. The United States is trying to rescue Russia, but Japan is not convinced that its national interests would be served by offering help.

That divergence is significant. In the wake of World War II, and with the coming of the Korean War, the United States and Japan struck a bargain, albeit an implicit one. The United States forgave all that Japan had done in World War II, and in return Japan became a loyal and dependable ally against the Communist bloc.

Although the new relationship was not forced upon Japan, it was a manifestly unequal one. In practical day-to-day terms it functioned much as the Lone Ranger–Tonto relationship. Many Japanese may be offended by the comparison, but the evidence is overwhelming. The roots of inequality go back to the very origins of the U.S.-Japanese relationship, when Commodore Matthew Perry demanded that Japan open up to the world. That "demander-demandee" pattern has persisted for more than a century. The Japanese remember well President Franklin D. Roosevelt's implicit demand that Japan withdraw from China, and Secretary of State John Foster Dulles's demand that Premier Yoshida Shigeru cease his efforts to normalize ties with China, both of which made President Richard Nixon's *shokku* decision to normalize ties with China — without consulting Japan — even more galling. Except on trade and economic issues, Japan has almost never said no to any significant U.S. demand since World War II, especially in the area of international security. Japan has also served as a vital banker for U.S. foreign policy goals, shaping its official development assistance policies to meet both U.S. and Japanese needs. Its long history of submitting to U.S. demands explains the appeal to the Japanese of Shintaro Ishihara's book *The Japan That Can Say No*, as well as the emergence of the new term *kenbei*, meaning dislike of the United States.

In recent times Japan has hesitated only once in responding to an important U.S. military demand, namely, that it contribute significantly to the Persian Gulf War. That hesitation was rooted in Japan's expectation that its oil supplies would not be affected by the Iraqi invasion of Kuwait, and in surprise that the West could abandon Saddam Hussein so soon after building him up as a Western asset. The Japanese public's aversion to direct participation in military conflict also played a part. That slowness to respond cost the Japanese dearly. Their reputation suffered badly in the United States, and even their payment of $13 billion, the largest single contribution from any non-Arab coalition member, did not alleviate the feeling that Japan had once again tried to be a free rider on the United States.

The decision of the U.S. government to use the U.S. media to pressure Japan publicly to supply some of the money, if not the men, to help in the Gulf War was a dangerous move on two counts. First, many

Americans already feel threatened by Japan's growing economic power. As Harvard political scientist Samuel Huntington put it, Americans are obsessed with Japan because they see it "as a major threat" to U.S. primacy in a crucial arena of power: economics. Many Americans, therefore, ask a commonsense question: Why should the United States spend money to defend a "free-riding" economic competitor? The media attention, then, further eroded U.S. support for the U.S.-Japanese relationship. It also reinforced the growing Japanese consensus that Americans are making Japan the scapegoat for their own domestic economic troubles. Objective analysis supports the Japanese contention that the root causes of the United States' economic problems lie in the failure of the U.S. government, in both the executive and legislative branches, to solve problems of its own creation: budget deficits, heavy internal and external borrowing, and the lack of sufficient long-term investment in either industry or the labor force, to cite just a few obvious points.

The admiration that the Japanese have genuinely felt for the United States, in part because it was unusually generous as an occupying power, is steadily diminishing. Japan is no longer prepared to be the "Tonto." In fact the Japanese increasingly perceive themselves to be superior to the "Lone Ranger." Thus, a structural change — from one-way condescension to mutual condescension — is taking place in the psychological relationship between Japan and the United States.

To prevent a breakdown in U.S.-Japanese relations, the Japanese establishment has consciously woven a thick web of economic interdependence between the two countries. However, even without a serious U.S.-Japanese rift, Japan could find itself abandoned. Fueled by perceptions of economic rivalry, U.S. relations with Japan could become friendly but merely normal — such as, for instance, U.S. relations with Switzerland. The United States would then no longer feel obliged to defend Japan or maintain forces in East Asia to protect Japan's sea lanes. Alternatively, close relations could fall victim to a resurgence of U.S. isolationism: "What we are concerned with is an America turning inward, politically and economically," said Takakazu Kuriyama, the Japanese ambassador to the United States. The Japanese fear that continued U.S. economic troubles — exacerbated by the U.S. government's inability to deal with them — would make Americans unwilling or unable to pay for a continued U.S. military overseas.

Difficult Neighbors

Deprived of the U.S. nuclear umbrella, Japan, the only country in the world to have experienced a nuclear attack, will feel threatened by its nuclear-equipped neighbors. What should the Japanese self-defense forces do if China implements its new law on the disputed Senkaku Islands and places troops there? Could a Chinese force be removed as easily as the symbolic Taiwanese presence was a few years ago? With its powerful economy, Japan currently towers over China, Korea, and Russia, but each raises unique security concerns. A hostile alliance of any two of those would be a strategic nightmare for a solitary Japan. With the new sense of uncertainty about the future viability of the U.S.-Japanese defense relationship, Japan has to take a fresh look at its relations with those three neighbors.

Of the three relationships the Russo-Japanese one appears to be the most troubled at present. The unresolved issue of the Kuril Islands continues to bedevil relations, but the troubled history of relations between Japan and Russia — including the brutal Soviet treatment of Japanese POWs and the USSR's last-minute entry into World War II against Japan, in violation of the treaty both had signed — aggravates Japanese distrust of the Russians. Even if the Kuril dispute is resolved, Japan has to ask itself whether long-term Japanese interests would be served by helping Russia become strong again.

Given the economic, social, and political mess that it finds itself in, Russia is not likely to threaten Japan in the near future; but a continuing cool Japanese attitude toward Russia could lead to problems with Japan's Western allies. In May 1992 German Chancellor Helmut Kohl publicly criticized Japan for not doing more to help Russia. The triumphant visit of Russian President Boris Yeltsin to Washington in June 1992 indicated that the United States is moving even closer to Russia. How long can Japan, a nominal member of the Western camp, buck that trend?

Traditionally the Japanese have viewed Korea as a "dagger pointed at the heart of Japan." In the past they have not hesitated to intervene in or invade Korea, leaving behind a rich residue of Korean distrust of Japan. Remarkably, forty-seven years after World War II, the Japanese have not even begun to reduce that distrust.

During the Cold War, Japan did not have to worry about Korea. The two large Korean armies threatened each other, not Japan. But if Korea reunifies, the succeeding Korean state, like united Germany, would inherit a formidable military capability, and it would be situated within striking distance of Japan. In 1992 the prospects of an early reunification do not look good — at least not until North Korean leader Kim Il Sung dies. But the outlines of the likely solution to the Korean problem are becoming clear. South Korea is likely to emerge as the successor state of the two Koreas, as West Germany did in reunified Germany.

The two powers that formerly guaranteed North Korean independence now show less interest in the continued division of Korea. Russia, as demonstrated by Mikhail Gorbachev's behavior, now even has a vested interest in a unified Korea dominated by South Korea, because that could enable Russia to play the "Korea card" against Japan. China's interests are not so clear-cut. The government in Beijing is probably not keen to see the disappearance of another ideological ally (although visitors to Beijing and Pyongyang can testify that those two cities seem to be in different ideological universes). However, the Chinese are remarkably pragmatic in their foreign policy; their concept of "flexible power" *(quan bian)* predates Machiavelli by centuries. If China's long-term interests favor a unified Korean peninsula, China will not hesitate to abandon an ideological ally. Japan should therefore assume that a unified Korea — with all the potential dangers that could bring — is in the making, even though the South Koreans, having watched West Germany's difficulties, favor a slower process of reunification.

Currently the Japanese are obsessed, and correctly so, with the threat that North Korea will develop nuclear weapons. They would not feel any less alarmed if South Korea inherited a nuclear capability. Given the traditional Japanese-Korean antipathy, several Japanese officials have confidentially said that while Japan can live with a nuclear-armed Russia and China, a nuclear-armed Korea would be unacceptable. Almost certainly Japan would build its own nuclear weapons in response.

The North Korean nuclear issue illustrates the complexity of the Northeast Asian security environment. The campaign against North Korea's nuclear development is publicly led by the United States and Japan. Yet China probably realizes that a North Korean nuclear capability could trigger the nuclearization of Japan. China knows that it cannot stop Japan from going nuclear on its own, and more crucially, it knows that only the United States can. Hence, even though China in principle opposes the U.S. military presence in the region, there is nothing that it dreads more than a U.S. military withdrawal that could induce Japan to acquire its own nuclear weapons.

Of the three, the most difficult relationship for Japan to work out in the post–Cold War era will ultimately be that with China. Unlike Russia, China cannot be treated purely as an adversary. Yet with the disappearance of the Soviet threat, and the perception that the United States may be turning inward, China and Japan are beginning to wonder whether they may not be left as the only two giant wrestlers in the ring. They have already begun to circle each other warily, each trying to ascertain the other's intentions.

For China the emergence of Japan has probably come as an unpleasant surprise. After Japan's surrender in World War II, its adoption of the peace constitution, and its servile dedication to U.S. foreign policy, China did not perceive Japan as either a threat or an equal. With its nuclear capability, its permanent seat on the United Nations Security Council, and the assiduous courtship it enjoyed from the United States and other Western countries during the Cold War, China clearly felt itself to be superior to Japan. It blithely ignored Japan's growing economic strength. Neither during Mao's lifetime nor after his death did China try to work out a long-term *modus vivendi* with Japan. Instead, its policies toward Japan have been offshoots of its other concerns; China used Japan to escape international isolation in the 1950s and again in the wake of Tiananmen.

Japan does not relish the idea of coming to terms with China on a one-to-one basis. For most of the Cold War, Japan looked up to China. Both Japan's surrender in World War II and the traditional relationship, in which Japan was a cultural and political satellite of China, made it easy for the Japanese to accept an unequal position. Today, however, they no longer respect China, perhaps not even culturally. Japanese leaders and officials have to disguise their disdain for China. They are especially contemptuous of the fact that more than one hundred years after the Meiji Restoration of 1868, when Japan began to institute reforms to meet the challenge of a technologically superior Western civilization, China still has not come to terms with the modern world.

In the short run Japan is primarily concerned that instability in China could bring a mass of refugees to Japan, the beginnings of which the Japanese have already experienced with the arrival of small Chinese fishing vessels. In the long run it fears that a successful China could once again overshadow Japan. Although at present the chances of that are slim, the Japanese recognize with awe the creativity and dynamism of Chinese scientists and entrepreneurs outside China. They see the birth of a new economic synergy linking Hong Kong and Taiwan to China. They realize that a well-organized China could leave Japan trailing, as the Tang dynasty did.

China holds the key to the solution of many of the region's pressing problems, such as those in Korea, Indochina, and Taiwan. Yet despite some common interests, Japan will probably find it unwise to raise those issues — except perhaps for Korea — with China. China would reject any discussion on Taiwan, which it considers to be an internal issue. The Chinese leadership would be deeply alarmed if a reduced U.S. presence in Asia brought closer political relations between Japan and Taiwan. So far, however, Japan has behaved with exquisite political correctness on the issue of Taiwan.

The Indochina issue illustrates the difficulty of working out a new Sino-Japanese modus vivendi. The Soviet collapse paved the way for the symbolic capitulation of Vietnam to China. China felt that it had reasserted its historical influence over the Indochinese peninsula. China, however, is in no position to help Vietnam extricate itself from its economic mess. Japan could help, but China would be deeply troubled by the prospect that Vietnam (or any Southeast Asian state) might be transformed into an economic satellite of Japan.

The potential for Sino-Japanese misunderstanding is great. As long as Beijing remains relatively isolated it will probably not do anything to provoke Japan. However, that relatively calm state of affairs may not last forever. China could emerge out of the cloud of Tiananmen. Japan's economic influence in the region could become even more pronounced. In the hope of "containing" that influence on China's periphery, some Chinese planners have already begun to think of a "small triangle" — composed of the United States, Japan, and China — to replace the "big triangle," which consisted of the United States, the USSR, and China. A new power structure is thus in the making. Despite the clear evidence that Japan will face new challenges in its relations with the United States and its neighbors, it will be psychologically difficult for the Japanese to admit that they face a problematic new strategic environment. They felt no immediate pain at the end of the Cold War. Instead, Japan appears to have been catapulted to a position of global eminence. Few greater gatherings of luminaries have been seen in recent times than at Emperor Hirohito's funeral.

The Forces of Drift
Even if the Japanese were to recognize the new challenges before them, five powerful forces will encourage continued drift.

First, restructuring the U.S.-Japanese relationship will be difficult. There is a great mismatch of needs, attitudes, perceptions, and power relations. Japan needs the United States for its security; the United States does not need Japan. Since Commodore Perry's time the United States has been used to making demands on Japan. Japan has never been in a position to make demands of its own. The Japanese see themselves as a tiny country overshadowed by a giant United States. But the American public also increasingly sees the Japanese as larger than life, providing the only real threat to continued U.S. economic predominance. Racial differences aggravate that sense of threat. The power imbalance can be demonstrated with an analogy. Washington sees the U.S.-Japanese relationship as a friendly game of chess. But where Washington sees it as a one-to-one game, Tokyo sees three other players on the same chessboard: China, Korea, and Russia. Any

Japanese move against the United States affects its ties with the other three. In Japanese eyes, there is no "level playing field" in the game.

Superficially there would appear to be no trouble in the security sphere. The United States has never expressed any doubts about its commitment to the Mutual Security Treaty (MST), notwithstanding the ongoing question of the cost of keeping U.S. troops in Japan. There is no American public debate on the treaty. "Why risk change?" is the attitude of Japanese policymakers. To restructure the relationship Japan will have to persuade the United States to continue to protect Japan and at the same time demand that the United States treat Japan as an equal partner. Asking for protection and parity in the same breath is never easy. It will be equally difficult for both sides to admit that while the form of the defense relationship will remain the same (meaning the MST will not be changed), the substance will be different. Instead of protecting Japan from the vanished Soviet threat, the treaty will restrain the nuclearization and militarization of Japan, consequently reassuring Japan's neighbors that it will remain peaceful. In short, the main purpose of the U.S.-Japanese MST will be to contain Japan's growth as a military power. The key problem will be, of course, arriving at such an understanding clearly and publicly, so that the American body politic understands and supports the MST, but without offending the Japanese people.

Second, if the Japanese admit to themselves that they face a new strategic environment with the long-term U.S. defense commitment in doubt, the fear is that the only obvious alternative to the MST is an independent Japanese military — and nuclear — capability. Japan is by no means a military midget. Its current defensive military capability is respected. However, without a nuclear umbrella and strong offensive capabilities, Japan cannot contemplate military confrontation with its nuclear-equipped neighbors. Some Japanese desire an independent nuclear capability, but they know that would set off global alarm bells. Many in the West have already developed an inferiority complex with regard to the Japanese and would be deeply troubled to see Japan extend its economic superiority into the military field. The West is not ready to accept the possibility that the preeminent power in all fields could be a non-Western country such as Japan, even though Japan is nominally a member of the "Western" group.

Third, if Japan tries to shift course and move closer to its neighbors it would have to abandon a century-old policy of believing that Japan's destiny lies with the West. Yukichi Fukuzawa, the great Meiji-era reformer, said that Japan should "escape from Asia, and enter into Europe." If it now reverses course and "enters" into Asia, some tensions could also develop with its Western partners. For example, since the end of the Cold War the promotion of democracy and human rights has been elevated in the Western scheme of priorities. Japan has gone along, by and large, though more out of convenience than conviction. However, as the West applies those new policies pragmatically on strategically important countries (Algeria, for example), and less pragmatically on less vital countries, the difference in geographical interests between Japan and the West will surface. Japan is well aware that a policy strongly based on the promotion of human rights would only invite several Asian countries to drag out the Japanese record up to the end of World War II. Thus Japan is caught between the devil and the deep blue sea in trying to balance its interests as a "Western" and also an Asian country. One more reason for drifting along.

Fourth, in order to review and reform its relations with its three neighbors, Japan will have to confront ghosts from the past that it has consciously ignored since World War II. To reshape its relations with both China and Korea, Japan must be able to look them squarely in the eye and acknowledge that it was responsible for some of the most painful chapters in their histories. Without such an acknowledgment it is hard to imagine how new bonds of trust could be forged. The Japanese have so far carefully and circumspectly expressed "regret" and "contrition," but, unlike the Germans, they have not yet brought themselves to apologize directly to those peoples.

As long as Emperor Hirohito was living, many Japanese felt constrained in discussing the issue of war crimes, because they wanted to avoid embarrassing him. The U.S. decision to ignore the atrocities committed by the Japanese during World War II in order to gain a strong ally in the Korean War deepened the silence around those matters by aggravating the natural tendency to avoid facing a painful topic. Many Japanese feel that the silence should continue, because what Japan did in Korea and China was no different from what Western colonizers did elsewhere, that the rape of Nanking was no different from the British massacre of Indian protesters at Amritsar. Why, they ask, should Japan atone for its colonial sins when the West never did so? But the Japanese ability to win the trust of their neighbors is linked to their own ability to acknowledge what happened. Many Japanese see a conspiracy to blacken Japan's name in any renewed discussion of World War II. They do not realize that it is an inevitable consequence of Japanese success. If Japan had remained like Bangladesh few would be interested in discussing its past. With its growing influence, however, it is natural that Japan's neighbors need reassurances that its newfound power will be exercised benignly.

Fifth, in attempting to chart a new course, Japan would also have to face its built-in cultural and political limitations. The Japanese have created a fairly harmonious society, but it is ethnocentric and exclusive. A foreigner has virtually no hope of being accepted as an equal member no matter how "Japanese" he or she may become in behavior. The inability (or unwillingness) of the Japanese to absorb the several hundred thousand Koreans who have lived in Japan for generations is a powerful statement of the exclusivity of Japanese society. Ethnic exclusivity, as demonstrated by South Africa, does not foster good neighborliness.

Those cultural obstacles are compounded by Japan's weak, divided, and scandal-ridden political leadership. The frequent changes of prime minister, the appointment of weak individuals to senior political positions, and the absence of visionary leaders for the new times have all compounded the country's inertia. Japanese behavior at Asia-Pacific Economic Cooperation Council meetings illustrates the problem. Unlike all the others, the Japanese delegation arrives with two heads, one from the ministry of international trade and industry and one from the foreign ministry. While it is not unusual for international delegations to include multiple agencies, it is unusual for one national delegation to speak with two voices. As a result, Japanese policy is often deadlocked, and the signals it sends are often mixed and confusing.

A New Regional Architecture

Despite these five reasons why Japan is likely to drift along, there are equally strong pressures upon Japan to set a bold new course in its foreign policy. The creation of a plethora of new committees, in both the ruling Liberal Democratic Party and the Parliament, demonstrates a new effervescence in Japanese thinking.

Japan's position as an "economic giant" but a "political dwarf" is no longer viable. Japan's economy is already larger than all other East Asian economies combined, and the Japanese GNP makes up 70 percent of the total for all of Asia, not counting the former Soviet republics. No European country enjoys such a position in its neighborhood. Only the United States comes close, in the size of its GNP compared to the Latin American economies. Yet Japan has relatively little political influence in East Asia — much less than the United States has in Latin America. To understand the anomalous position of Japan in East Asia, imagine the United States having less political influence in Latin America than either Brazil or the countries of the Andean Pact. That is Japan's current position in East Asia in relation to China or the Association of South-East Asian Nations (ASEAN). That situation cannot endure.

Japan's problem is that it must create a new political architecture for the region — from scratch. History does not help. The only traditional precolonial political architecture of the region rested on the concept of the "Middle Kingdom," whereby East and Southeast Asia paid tribute to Beijing. Japan cannot re-create such an arrangement. Nor can China, given its current weakness. In forging a new architecture Japan will find that it must construct at least five pillars.

The first pillar must be a reaffirmation of Japan's non-nuclear status. Japanese leaders may privately consider it unfair that Japan is still not trusted with nuclear weapons, yet they know that a decision by Japan to acquire nuclear weapons would destabilize all of its gains since World War II: Japan would find itself isolated not just from its three neighbors but also from the West. That would be nothing short of a strategic nightmare. A strong (rather than grudging) reaffirmation of the non-nuclear option would enhance its neighbors' confidence that Japan's intentions are peaceful. In this light, the continuing rejection of militarism by the Japanese public should also be seen as a strength rather than a weakness, because it assuages the fears of Japan's neighbors.

The second pillar of the new architecture must be a restructured U.S.-Japanese relationship. Fundamentally, Japan has to ask itself whether allowing the U.S.-Japanese relationship to continue to drift on its present course will naturally lead to stronger and closer bonds between the two countries, or whether the continuation of the present pattern — in which the Japanese public feels constantly bullied by the United States and the American public sees Japan as a "free rider" growing wealthy at the United States' expense — will bring a progressive deterioration.

So far Japan has concentrated its efforts on enhancing the economic interdependence between the two countries, acting as a banker for U.S. foreign policy, accepting U.S. vetoes of Japanese foreign policy initiatives, and making it affordable for the Pentagon to station military forces in Japan by paying half the cost. In private the Japanese often see the United States as a temperamental bull that has to be appeased from time to time. But since the U.S. government has expressed no desire to change the relationship, Japanese planners might wonder, why risk change? Yet the Japanese need to be aware of the profoundly democratic nature of American society. The commitment of the U.S. government to defend Japan is real only if it has the support of the American people. Japan cannot afford to make the same mistake the South Vietnamese generals did in 1975 when they accepted at face value Washington's commitment to defend Saigon without paying attention to American public opinion.

Today Japan has to convince both the U.S. government and the American people that the U.S.-Japanese security relationship is in the interest of both countries; that Japan is no free rider; and that its commitment to a non-nuclear strategy serves the interests of the United States, the West, and the region. After all, if the United States abandons the MST, U.S. defense planners will have many new concerns. If Japan goes nuclear the United States will have to plan a defense against a nuclear power that, unlike the USSR, could be technologically more advanced than the United States. Japan could also pose new competition for American arms exporters, an area Japan has not ventured into so far.

The economic tensions between the two countries must also be addressed squarely. The United States has to admit publicly that Japan is being made the scapegoat for the former's inability to get its own economic house in order. For its part, Japan needs to state unequivocally that a strong United States is in the interest of Japan and the Asia-Pacific region as a whole and that it will work with its neighbors in formulating economic policies to enhance both U.S. competitiveness and U.S. economic interests in the region. Such a clear statement, followed by concrete actions, might help lay to rest a growing sentiment in the United States that Japan is weakening the U.S. economy.

There is a seeming contradiction between Japan's need for continued U.S. protection and its desire to stand up for itself. But that contradiction arises out of the peculiar nature of the U.S.-Japanese relationship, in which a giant economic power is not allowed to have nuclear weapons. If Japan could become a nuclear power it could behave like France or the United Kingdom toward the United States; but because that is not an option, the United States should allow Japan to spread its influence in other spheres and not remain a satellite of U.S. foreign policy.

The third pillar of Japan's new architecture must be the development of good-neighbor policies with China, Korea, and Russia. Recent history in Western Europe has demonstrated that long-held animosities need not endure. While Britain, France, and Germany first joined together under pressure of the common Soviet threat, they are now held together by the immensely intricate networks forged between their societies. Japan can replicate such networks with its neighbors. Trade and investment flows are leading the way; in their wake the Japanese should seek to foster greater cross-cultural understanding. Southeast Asia has long been described as the Balkans of Asia. The many races, languages, cultures, and religions approximate the Balkans in their variety; they have helped form a history that is equally complex and sad. Despite those obstacles, the ASEAN countries have managed to forge the most successful regional cooperation of the Third World.

Tokyo can do no less if it undertakes bold initiatives such as resolving the islands dispute with Russia and apologizing to the Korean and Chinese peoples for the horrors of the past. The Japanese have great psychological difficulties in accepting the need for an apology, but they should realize that just as they will never be able to trust the Russians until Moscow apologizes for the brutal treatment of Japanese POWs after World War II, their neighbors, too, need an apology from their former enemies in Tokyo.

The fourth pillar must be to build some sense of a common Asian home. Europe was able to escape the legacy of centuries of rivalries and animosities by creating a feeling of a common European home, long before Gorbachev uttered that phrase, with a common Greco-Roman heritage serving as a foundation. The ultimate challenge faced by the Japanese is to try to achieve a similar sense in East Asia. Only a common perception that all are riding in the same boat will prevent the region from dissolving into bitter and dangerous conflict. Perhaps the example of the Chinese, Japanese, Korean, and other East Asian communities in Los Angeles, who decided to forget their differences and work together after the recent riots, could have an influence on their parent countries.

Creating such a sense of a common Asian home will be another difficult psychological shift for the Japanese. Ever since the Meiji Restoration they have equated success with Western acceptance. Clearly, though, to earn the long-term trust of its Asian neighbors — especially giants such as China, India, and Indonesia — Japan has to demonstrate that it respects them as fellow Asian countries. It must not treat them with the condescension they sometimes encounter in the West. Japanese aid policies, for example, cannot be simple extensions of Western aid policies, if only because Japan has different geographical interests. In dealing with Asia, Japan has so far acceded almost reflexively to U.S. or Western interests, although neither the United States nor Japan will admit to any coercion. For example, when Malaysia suggested an East Asian economic grouping, Japan acquiesced to U.S. opposition before considering whether the region would benefit from such an organization. Similarly, following the Cambodian peace agreement, Japan wanted to lift its investment embargo on Vietnam and end the Asian Development Bank moratorium on loans to Vietnam. But here, too, it gave in to the U.S. position.

The United States does not hesitate in making such demands of Japan, asserting its rights as a protector. Yet wiser counsel should prevail in Washington. The United States should stop asking Japan to fashion its policies primarily to defend U.S. interests; that will not work in the long run. U.S. opposition to new multilateral links in the Asia-Pacific region clearly illustrates the shortsightedness of U.S. policies. With the explosive growth in trade and investment among the East Asian societies, there is a great need for strengthened multilateral links to lubricate those contacts and provide venues for resolving common problems among the East Asian countries.

Any serious consideration of a common Asian home evokes great disquiet in the United States and in the West generally, mostly for fear that another exclusive racial club is being formed. That reflects Western ignorance of the enormous racial and cultural divisions within Asia. The main function of a common Asian home (to include Australia and New Zealand), like the common European home, would be to reduce or dissolve racial identities, not to enhance them.

Finally, the fifth pillar requires Japan to become a good global citizen. Japan's efforts to gain a permanent seat on the UN Security Council reflect that desire. However, its method of trying to gain that seat is a classic case of putting the cart before the horse. Without an established track record of managing international conflicts, what would Japan do on the Security Council? Japan's case for a permanent seat would clearly be enhanced if Tokyo could demonstrate, as the United States has in the Middle East, that it can take the lead in resolving international conflicts.

Consider, for example, the Cambodian peace process. An excellent peace agreement has been signed, but its implementation has been hobbled by a lack of funding, with the United States finding it hard to raise its share of the cost of UN peacekeeping operations. If they follow tradition, the Japanese will wait for the U.S. government to approach them for financial assistance and, after some hesitation, agree to the U.S. request. Instead, the Japanese government should take the initiative and announce that it will meet any financial shortfall in the Cambodian UN operations, thus taking the lead in meeting the economic reconstruction needs of Cambodia. Japan should declare that it will ensure that the long nightmare of the Cambodian people is finally over, fulfilling its responsibilities to both the region and common humanity. The entire operation would cost Japan $1 billion or $2 billion, a fraction of what it paid for the Gulf War, yet the kudos that Japan could earn — in the region, in the West, and especially in the United States — would be enormous. Such a move could drastically alter public perceptions of the Japanese as mere calculating beings with no moral purpose. That is the sort of bold leap that Japan needs to make.

Bold steps, of course, have not been the hallmark of Japanese foreign policy since World War II. Caution has been the key word. But a new transpacific crisis is in the making. Fortunately both the dangers and the opportunities are clear. The East Asian region is experiencing perhaps the most spectacular economic growth in human history. It began with Japan and spread throughout the region. Yet all East Asian governments realize that even now their countries' economic growth would be crippled if Japan were to falter. Japan, therefore, will have considerable influence in the fashioning of a new political architecture for the region. However, to succeed, it will have to meet the interests not only of Japan, but also of its three immediate neighbors, of the East Asian region generally, and of the United States. The future will severely test the diplomatic vision and skill of Japan's leaders.

"THE PACIFIC IMPULSE"

*In September 1994 I gave an opening address at the 36th Annual Conference
of the International Institute of Strategic Studies, held in Vancouver.
The conference brought together mainly American and European strategic
thinkers. The natural assumption in these strategic minds was that Europe
was ahead of the rest of the world in strategic theory and practice, that the
key concepts and paradigms had been worked out in Europe, and that the
rest of the world could do no better than emulate Europe. My lecture shocked
the audience on two counts: first, I suggested that the Asia-Pacific, not Europe,
had better prospects for peace; second, I suggested that the ways of the Pacific
may provide an alternative* Weltanschauung *for strategic thinkers. The
response was clearly hostile. But when excerpts from my speech were published
in* Foreign Affairs *(as "The Pacific Way") and* Survival *(as "The Pacific
Impulse"), they drew a kinder response. Gareth Evans, then the Australian
foreign minister, told me that he had quoted me in his speeches, especially
my suggestion that the Asia-Pacific would unleash a burst of explosive
creativity with the fusion of Asian and American civilizations.*

*Six years later my thesis has gone through a wrenching test. The
1997–98 Asian Financial Crisis was one of the greatest economic crises
of the twentieth century. The havoc it created among many East Asian
economies was enormous. Western thinkers have often pointed out that
economic crises, coupled with major power shifts, have often led to war, as
they did with World War II.*

*No other region in the world is experiencing power shifts of the scale we
are seeing today in the Asia-Pacific theater. This theater is also full of geopolitical fault lines: Russia-Japan, Japan-China, China–South China Sea,
not to mention the most important emerging strategic relationship in the
world: the U.S.-China relationship.*

Why then has the region remained at peace through these wrenching times? Why have tensions not resurfaced? All I can say is that six years after writing this essay, I feel vindicated in some of the claims I have made about "The Pacific Impulse." It is alive, not dead. Nevertheless, skeptics abound. Most Western strategic thinkers continue to believe that the Asia-Pacific theater remains a powder keg waiting to blow. Only time will tell who is right. For the sake of my children and grandchildren (if I have any), I hope that I am.

THE TWENTY-FIRST CENTURY WILL SEE A STRUGGLE between an "Atlantic impulse" and a "Pacific impulse." For the past few centuries the Atlantic impulse has determined the course of world history. If my assumptions are right and the Pacific impulse takes center stage over the Atlantic impulse, then Eurocentric strategic analysts will have to rethink their concepts and assumptions to understand the future flow of history.

The twenty-first century will be unique, because there will be three centers of world power (Europe, North America, and East Asia) as opposed to two in the twentieth century (Europe and North America) and one in the immediate preceding centuries (Europe). In previous centuries Europe set the course of world history: it colonized most parts of the world, shook up other empires and societies (including China, Japan, and the Islamic world), and occupied relatively empty spaces (North America and Australasia) through immigration. The two world wars of the twentieth century, and even the Cold War that succeeded them, were essentially pan-European struggles. East Asia, by contrast, had little impact on the rest of the world.

It would be dangerous for both Europe and mankind if analysts were unable to liberate themselves from Eurocentric conceptions of the world. Like all other parts of the world that have experienced greatness, Europe too is becoming exhausted. The time has come for other regions to contribute as much as Europe has in moving the world forward.

The Rise of East Asia

In the twenty-first century East Asia will shed its passivity. The region's sheer economic weight will give it a voice and a role. As recently as

1960 Japan and East Asia together represented 4 percent of the world's GNP, while the United States, Canada, and Mexico represented 37 percent. Today the two areas have a similar proportion of the world's GNP (some 23–24 percent), but with more than half of the world's economic growth taking place in Asia in the 1990s, the North Atlantic Free Trade Agreement (NAFTA) and European economies will progressively become (relatively) smaller.[1] Initially it will be the economic weight of East Asia that will have the most significant impact. This may explain why European economists and industrialists treat East Asia with respect, while, by contrast, ideologues and strategists, seeing no vigorous intellectual challenge from East Asia, believe that they have little to learn from the region.

Almost all strategic analysts assume that only the European experience can explain East Asia's future. And in the inevitable comparisons with Europe, East Asia always comes out second best. Richard Betts says, "One of the reasons for optimism about peace in Europe is the apparent satisfaction of the great powers with the status quo," while in East Asia there is "an ample pool of festering grievances, with more potential for generating conflict than during the Cold War, when bipolarity helped stifle the escalation of parochial disputes."[2] And according to Aaron L. Friedberg, "While civil war and ethnic strife will continue for some time to smoulder along Europe's peripheries, in the long run it is Asia that seems far more likely to be the cockpit of great-power conflict. The half millennium during which Europe was the world's primary generator of war (as well as wealth and knowledge) is coming to a close. But, for better or for worse, Europe's past could be Asia's future."[3] Barry Buzan and Gerald Segal, after reviewing the history of conflict in East Asia, wrote:

All of these historical legacies remain and, taken together, they suggest political fragmentation and hostility characterising the region's international relations. There is little that binds its states and societies together but much that divides them. Any chance of finding unifying common ground against the West has long since disappeared. As the particular distortions imposed by the

Cold War unravel, many historical patterns that were either suppressed or overridden by ideological and superpower rivalry are reappearing. . . . History, therefore, strongly reinforces the view that Asia is in danger of heading back to the future.[4]

Many Asians fear that such passages do not merely contain analytical predictions, but that they also represent Europe's hope that East Asia will not succeed and surpass it.

The Tidal Wave

What is striking about the above articles is a blindness to the biggest tidal wave to hit East Asia, which is the fundamental reason for the region's economic dynamism: the tidal wave of common sense and confidence. Over the past decade or two an immense psychological revolution has occurred and is continuing in most East Asian minds: increasing numbers realize that they have wasted centuries trying and failing to make it into the modern world. They can no longer afford to fail. After centuries, their moment has come. Why waste it on relatively petty disputes or historical squabbles?

It is difficult for a European or North American to understand the momentous nature of this psychological revolution, because they cannot step into East Asian minds. Their minds have never been wrapped in the cellophane of colonialism. They have never had to struggle with the subconscious assumption that perhaps they are second-rate human beings, never good enough to be "number one." The growing realization among East Asians that they can match, if not better, other cultures and societies has led to an explosion of confidence.

This confidence is further bolstered by their awareness that the time needed to catch up with the developed world is getting progressively shorter. The period that nations take to double their output per head is shortening — the United Kingdom took 58 years (from 1780), the United States 47 years (from 1839), Japan 33 years (from the 1880s), Indonesia 17 years, South Korea 11 years, China 10 years. The reasons are complex, but they include the faster spread of technology, ideas, and business practices, and of course the rapid movement of capital across borders.

Many East Asians are also increasingly aware that they are doing some fundamental things correctly in their societies, in contrast to many European societies. Many European thinkers celebrate the firm implantation of democracies in their societies as an unmitigated good, especially since it prevents wars. But democratic systems can also be deeply resistant to change. The heavy welfare burdens accumulated by Europe cannot be shed easily, especially since the burden is often passed to future generations. The American Bureau of the Budget recently forecast that for an American infant born this year, the tax requirement to pay for existing programs will be 82 percent of his lifetime earnings. William Rees-Mogg notes that "this figure is obviously unsupportable," but adds that "government spending in Europe is actually higher than it is in the US."[5]

Several of Europe's socioeconomic policies are fundamentally untenable. Since 1977 Europe has created only 9 million jobs compared to 30 million in the United States and Canada. During this period most of the jobs created in the U.S. were in the private sector, while in Europe they were in the public sector. As a consequence, taxation in Europe is increasing and the social cost linked to wages is, on average, twice that of the United States.[6]

Some forecasts already indicate a 1 percent annual drop in real European disposable income over the next twenty-five years. A European child born today faces the prospect of earning less than his parents. By contrast, East Asians are aware that they are about to be carried up by a huge rising tide. This year the total gross domestic product (GDP), in real purchasing-power terms, of the 2.5 billion people in China, India, Japan, and the Asian Rim is probably about half that of the 800 million in Europe and North America. By 2025 the Asian GDP will be double that of the Euro-American.[7]

More than one hundred years ago Japan was the first Asian society to attempt to enter the modern world, with the Meiji Restoration. Decades of military conflict followed, with some initial successes in the Sino-Japanese and the Russo-Japanese wars, then disaster and ignominy. Is it not conceivable that one hundred years later East Asia could follow the same path: economic modernization leading eventually to military conflict and disaster?

But there is something crucially different between what Japan tried to do a hundred years ago and what East Asia is attempting now. Japan believed fervently that it could become successful only if it joined the premier club of the world then: the club of colonizers. As Richard J. Samuels says, "Japan's early industrialisation was led by military industries to enhance national security by 'catching up and surpassing the West.'" This mobilization was captured by the slogan "Rich Nation, Strong Army" (fukoku kyohei).[8] Economic modernization was not a goal in itself, but was, as shown by Europe in the preceding century or two, a stepping-stone to military conquest.

The dynamic in East Asia today could not be more different from the environment Japan experienced in the later nineteenth century. East Asia is trying to achieve something much more fundamental: it wants to succeed in its own right, without trying to become a member of a European club. It will be an immense struggle to work out social, political, and philosophical norms that best capture their people's aspirations, but it will also be an all-engrossing struggle. The most foolish thing that any East Asian society could do is to turn away from this overwhelming challenge and engage in traditional military rivalries: to once more snatch failure from the jaws of victory.

Comparing Geostrategic Environments: Europe and East Asia

Conventional European thinkers are likely to be unmoved by this picture of a great human drama unfolding in East Asia. They focus their strategic sights either on ancient and smoldering rivalries or on arms races. As indicated above, conventional wisdom suggests that East Asia, in contrast to Europe, is likely to experience a much less benign strategic environment.

Barry Buzan and Gerald Segal reinforce this point by looking at the role of what they call "international society" in maintaining international peace and stability. As they say: "International society encompasses the more specific notion of regimes. It suggests a situation in which a whole set of regimes, multilateral organisations and rules exists that enables states to communicate on a regular basis, to establish modes and habits of consultation and cooperation, to coordinate and manage their relations, and to prevent their disputes escalating into conflict or war." They add, "Europe, in particular, and the West, in general, constitute advanced and richly developed international societies. What is distinctive about Asia is its combination of several industrialised societies with a regional international society so impoverished in its development that it compares poorly with even Africa and the Middle East."[9]

Such conventional wisdom, however, fails to acknowledge one fundamental fact: in East Asia the guns are quiet, while Europe is surrounded by a ring of fire that burns in Algeria, ripples through North Africa, surfaces again in the vicious fighting in Bosnia, and reaches a climax in the Caucasus. From the conflict in Georgia to the explosions waiting to burst in Kosovo, Macedonia, and Albania, more lives are lost daily on the periphery of Europe than in the entire Asia-Pacific region, which has a much larger population.

In comparing East Asia with Europe, several writers stress that the presence of developed regional institutions, such as the North Atlantic Treaty Organization (NATO), the European Union (EU) and the Organization on Security and Cooperation in Europe (OSCE), gives Europe a competitive advantage in peace and security. OSCE has even been suggested as a model for the Asia-Pacific region. But of the fifty-three members of OSCE, the following are experiencing either internal or external conflicts: Serbia, Croatia, Bosnia, Armenia, Azerbaijan, Georgia, Moldova, and Tajikistan, not to mention the conflict brewing in Macedonia and Kosovo. The silence of the guns in the Asia-Pacific and the roar of the guns around Europe is not an accident but a result of the fact that Europe's approach to its immediate environment is strategically incoherent, while East Asia is making relatively sound strategic decisions.

There are several flawed elements in Europe's policies. The first is its belief that it can secure peace by concentrating on the internal unification of Europe while remaining detached from its periphery. To an observer from East Asia, all the efforts to deepen unification through the Maastricht Treaty or widen unification by incorporating "similar" European countries into the European Union seem like a household working to rearrange the living-room furniture while ignoring the floodwaters seeping in from the rising tides just outside the door. It is puzzling that Europe is trying to draw up its ramparts to cut itself off from its neighbors — excluding them from its growth and prosperity and keeping them as outsiders. In contrast, the strategic impulse in East Asia is to draw all societies into the region's dynamism, starting with Myanmar and Vietnam and eventually including North Korea.

Europe has no choice but to deal with three major forces on its doorstep: Russia, Africa, and Islam. In a shrinking world, the turbulence in these three areas will seep into Europe. While Europe has had a marginally successful strategy toward Russia (questions remain about its long-term viability), it has had a fundamentally flawed strategy toward Africa and Islam.

From a long-term perspective it may have been a strategic error for Europe to admit socially and culturally similar states into the EU ahead of Turkey. It sent a signal that Europe would always be cut off from the world of Islam: that no state in the Islamic world, no matter how secular, modernized, or "European," would be admitted into the "house of Europe." An opportunity was lost to demonstrate that an Islamic society could cross cultural boundaries and be like any other modern European state. Europe may also have lost a valuable opportunity to demonstrate that it can transcend its cultural boundaries and create region-wide institutions, as the Asia-Pacific has done in setting up such bodies as the Association of Southeast Asian Nations (ASEAN), the Asia-Pacific Economic Cooperation Conference (APEC), and the ASEAN Regional Forum (ARF), which contain a wide variety of cultures.

This exclusion of the Islamic world has been magnified by European passivity in the face of genocide at its doorstep in Bosnia. Few in the Islamic world (or elsewhere) believe that Europe would have been as passive if Muslim artillery shells had been raining down on Christian populations in Sarajevo or Srebrenica. It does not help that Europe condemns the reversal of democracy in Myanmar while endorsing a similar reversal in Algeria. Such double standards are easily shrugged off by cynical Europeans. But they underestimate the enormous price Europe is paying in alienating a force, Islam, that it will have to live with for the next thousand years. For the past few decades one of Europe's greatest strengths has been its moral leadership: often providing the right moral responses and massive humanitarian assistance in major crises. Gradually European leaders are waking up to the magnitude of the problem. German Chancellor Helmut Kohl asserted this year that "the rise of Islamic fundamentalism in North Africa is the major threat" to Europe, while Prime Minister Edouard Balladur of France has called the fundamentalist revolution in Algeria the leading threat to his country.[10]

A second flawed element in European strategy is the assumption that the rest of the world, including its neighbors, will follow the European social idea — that the natural progression of history will lead all societies to become liberal-democratic and capitalist. For most Europeans this assumption was vindicated when Russian President Mikhail Gorbachev followed this path. The Soviet Union's subsequent collapse and disappearance further vindicated it. Hence it was natural that so many Europeans embraced the idea that "the end of history" had come with the universal applicability of the Western idea.

This profound belief in the superiority of the Western idea creates a unique weakness or blindness in Europe: an inability to accept the simple notion that other cultures or societies may have equal validity. An essay entitled "Islam and the West" in the *Economist* demonstrates this blindness.[11] The article assumes that for Islamic societies to progress they must become more like the West. Not once does it suggest that the West might have something to learn from Islam. Again, to suggest a simple contrast, both the world's most populous Islamic state (Indonesia) and the world's most economically successful Islamic state (Malaysia) are in the Asia-Pacific. There is no suggestion in the region that they should follow some other model. This belief in the universality of the Western idea can block the acceptance of the principle of diversity and prevent a region from living in peace with other cultures. The Asia-Pacific is used to diversity, but Europe is not.

A third flawed element in European strategy is its effort to "lock in" the relatively high living standards of Europe by raising new barriers to free trade and sustaining high subsidies. Here the contrast between the strategies of the United States and Europe is striking. The United States has taken the relatively bold leap of crossing a cultural as well as a socioeconomic divide by entering into a free-trade agreement with Mexico. Effectively it had no choice, because if it did not export some low-paying jobs to Mexico and gain high-paying jobs in return (in a "win-win" arrangement), Mexico could not and would not stop exporting its populace into the United States.

The only permanent solution to the inevitable long-term problem of illegal immigration into Europe is to export some low-paying jobs (in return for high-paying jobs) and enter into free-trade agreements, initially with North Africa. In the long run this strategy is more likely to work if Europe promotes (rather than hinders) global free-trade regimes that will integrate Europe and its neighbors into the rising tide of prosperity in the Asia-Pacific. But to allow Europe's neighbors to compete in their areas of natural comparative advantage, European agricultural subsidies have to be abolished. It is quite frightening that such a simple, sensible solution to Europe's long-term strategic problem is considered virtually impossible.

In 1990 the ratio of Europe's population to Africa's was 498 million to 642 million; according to United Nations projections, by 2050, based on medium fertility extension, the ratio will be 486 million to 2.27 billion — a ratio akin to the white-black ratio in today's South Africa. Within a few decades Western Europe will be confronted with impoverished masses on its borders, and increasing numbers will be slipping in to join the millions already there.[12] Unless these masses feel that they are a part of European prosperity in their homelands, they will feel no choice but to move into the "house of Europe."

Some writers are beginning to recognize that Africa is Europe's problem. William Pfaff recently asked, "Who is responsible for the African catastrophe?" and answered, "The European powers, who colonized Africa in the nineteenth century out of an immensely complex mixture of good and bad motives, thereby destroying Africa's existing social and political systems, its customary institutions and law." He then asked, "Who outside Africa has an urgent material interest in Africa's salvation?" and his answer was, "The Europeans.

Besides the fact that Europe is the principal consumer of African mineral and agricultural exports, Africa's foundering means that hundreds of thousands, even millions more desperate people are attempting to get out of Africa to places where they can find order, jobs, security, a future. Their scarcely controllable migration towards Europe already has created immense social problems and serious political tensions."[13]

These flawed elements in European strategy mean a similar impulse is being exported to the rest of the world. I call this the "Atlantic impulse": moving toward continental unification rather than global integration; and exporting political development ahead of economic development, while ignoring social and cultural differences and creating new protectionist barriers to "lock in" untenable welfare-state policies. If Europe persists with the Atlantic impulse, it will be a loss not only for Europe, but also for the rest of the world, which has benefited so much from European creativity and dynamism.

A Concrete Example of the Atlantic Impulse

The Uruguay Round (UR) of the General Agreement on Tariffs and Trade (GATT) negotiations, which was deadlocked from 1989 to 1993 because of European intransigence, illustrates how the Atlantic impulse can damage global interests. It would probably have ended in disaster if not for the crucial APEC leaders' meeting in Seattle in November 1993. The United States cleverly sent a signal that if the UR broke down, it would have no choice but to create an Asia-Pacific free-trade area or regime. The other APEC leaders supported this message, and after a few critical phone calls between Bonn and Paris, Europe finally decided to sign the UR agreements in December 1993.

It was then decided that the final signing ceremony would be held in Marrakesh, Morocco. Unfortunately the location of this city, close to the Atlantic, led to the surfacing of the Atlantic impulse through an event that almost undermined the final agreement. After gaining the APEC countries' support to secure European approval of the UR agreement, the United States suddenly switched sides and teamed up with Europe to try to incorporate the "social clause" into the agreement. The social clause is ostensibly designed to improve working conditions in the Third World. Many Europeans defend it as representing a moral impulse. In doing so they insult the intelligence of the rest of the world, who find it hard to accept that the Europeans are morally interested in the fate of these workers now that their incomes are rising but were not interested when their incomes were stagnant. The social clause is a charade that will not be of any benefit to Europe.

Working with the Europeans caused the United States to suffer, because it was poorly received by its APEC partners, a point that some gracious U.S. officials admit in private. But this whole episode had even greater significance. It demonstrated that the United States, given its geographical location, will be torn between the Atlantic and Pacific impulses for decades to come. Over the next ten years American choices will probably be the most pivotal factor in international relations.

The United States: Atlantic or Pacific First?

During the Cold War the geopolitical environment of the United States was clear. The threat came from the Soviet Union, and the Atlantic alliance was the most important security priority. When victory came, the then secretary of state, James Baker, captured the sweetness of the moment by declaring the creation of a community stretching from Vancouver to Vladivostok (a circle that virtually covered the whole world except the intervening Pacific Ocean). It was probably the finest moment for the Atlantic impulse.

The interests that will link the United States across the Atlantic and Pacific Oceans, to Europe and East Asia respectively, will increasingly diverge. Culturally, the United States will look to Europe for its roots. The political and military institutions will also remain stronger across the Atlantic: institutions as varied as the Group of Seven (G-7), the OSCE, NATO, and the Organization for Economic Cooperation and Development (OECD) will attract American leaders across the Atlantic. These links will endure.

But the economic and perhaps the overall national security of the United States will be determined increasingly by developments across the Pacific. Last year, transpacific trade totaled $330 billion — 50 percent greater than transatlantic trade. The ratio will reach 2 to 1 by the end of this decade.

There is no doubt where the future growth markets are. By incorporating four more states into the European Union in January 1995, the EU will add 29 million consumers. Even if the larger Eastern European states (Czech Republic, Slovakia, Hungary, and Poland) are included, there will be an increase of 65 million consumers. In contrast, in East Asia alone there are 1,840 million consumers, and as greater numbers of them reach the critical benchmark of $1,000 per capita per year, their demand for consumer products grows. And immediately beyond East Asia is India, with a soaring middle class (200 million now and 400 million within a decade) and upper class (40 million).

The eyes of strategic thinkers glaze over when consumer products are discussed rather than nuclear proliferation. But major strategic decisions are influenced by consumer markets. In June 1994 the United States finally lifted a major cloud hanging over the Asia-Pacific region by de-linking China's most-favored-nation (MFN) status from nontrade issues. The critical factor in this decision was the potential size of China's consumer market. (It appears to have been the strong and determined leadership of the United States that defused the North Korean nuclear crisis. Future historians will record that ultimately even leaders such as Kim Il Sung and Kim Jong Il were conditioned by regional dynamics not to behave like Saddam Hussein.)

But economics alone will not draw the United States closer to the Pacific. The larger sociopolitical and military-security environments, as well as cultural comfort, are equally crucial factors. There is a deeply held belief among European strategic thinkers, as well as among the Atlanticists who live close to the Atlantic shores of the United States, that the United States will trade across the Pacific but be a member of the Atlantic community. Indeed, even the idea of a Pacific community is dismissed because of the diversity and cleavages in the region.

It may therefore be useful to discuss what a possible Pacific community would look like and how it would differ from the Atlantic community. It will come as a surprise to many Europeans to learn that a vision of such a community is already emerging, and more important, that some of the initial foundations have already been laid. And this, in turn, explains why the Pacific impulse is increasing in the United States day by day.

The Pacific Community: A Vision

There has never been anything like a Pacific community before. Hence those who try to discern the future of the Pacific from its past will be blind to its possibilities. It will be unlike anything that existed before, because it will be neither an Asian community nor an American community. The Pacific has the potential to become the most dynamic region in the world, because it can bring together the best from several streams of rich civilizations in Asia and the West, and if the fusion works the creativity could be on a scale never seen or experienced before.

There has already been some such creativity. The dynamism of East Asia is not purely a renaissance of rich ancient cultures: it is the result of a successful fusion of East and West in the reconstruction of their societies. Japan has already demonstrated what success such a formula can bring. Culturally it remains quintessentially Japanese, but its civil administration (with arguably the most powerful "Westernized" rational bureaucracy in the world), business, science, and technology are among the best in the world. It has modernized and is no longer a feudal society (several key imperial ceremonies are conducted in tailcoats, and Japan has one of the most Europeanized courts in the world), but the Japanese remain Japanese. While many Japanese teenagers look superficially like their European or American counterparts, their homes are Japanese, their souls are Japanese, and they are reverential toward their elders. And there is relatively little juvenile delinquency or crime. The deep glue that holds Asian societies and families together has not been eroded by modernization.

The result, in the eyes of many, is an economic and industrial miracle. Japanese productivity in most manufacturing sectors cannot be matched by any other workforce in the world. But this success is due neither to Japanese culture nor to Western methods: it is a result of the combination of the two.

This is why the efforts of American trade negotiators to create a "level playing field" by juggling with trade rules and regimes is seen by many in Asia to be a futile exercise. On a totally level playing field, most Japanese industries will outperform their American counterparts (even though there will be many areas in which the United States will continue to excel). Kenneth Courtis pointed out in an address to the Pacific Basin Economic Council of Canada on 18 April 1994: "For example, in 1993, in its third year of the most difficult recession of the past four decades, Japan committed 18.2 percent of its GNP to capital investment. In contrast, the figure was only 12 percent of GNP for the United States. At the peak of an investment-led GNP expansion last year Japan invested some $5,777 per capita in new plants and equipment, while America invested $2,519 per capita." In the long run the United States will be able to match Japan when it undergoes a parallel process of osmosis: absorbing the best of Asian civilizations as East Asia has been absorbing the best of the West.

The real success of the Pacific community will come when the learning process in the region becomes a two-way, rather than a one-way, street. It took a long time for China and other East Asian societies to accept the sensible advice of Yukichi Fukuzawa, the Meiji reformer, "to progress and learn from the West." An American, William Smith Clark, is worshiped in Sapporo, because he inspired young Japanese with his remark "Boys, be ambitious." When an American town proclaims a Japanese (or any other East Asian) as a hero, it will mark the arrival of a two-way street of ideas.

Some progress, however, has been made. Japanese quality-control methods (which were conceived by an American, Arthur Demming) have begun to be transplanted to America. The American car industry is finally eager to learn from Japan, and the United States is now keen to study Japanese methods in specific industrial fields.

Real learning requires humility. Fortunately the Americans are fundamentally an open and compassionate people. They carry no hubris from history, as the Europeans do. Only this can explain why the United States has been the most benevolent great power in history. European nations with such power would have used it to advance only their own national interests. Americans pushed an idea. And they have contributed to uplifting East Asian society. East Asia would not be where it is today if it had not been for the generosity of the Sterling Fashion American spirit. With each passing day the bright young East Asian minds driving the economic effervescence of the region increasingly come from American universities. The United States provides the bridges for the fusion of East and West in the Pacific.

History demonstrates that trade brings with it not just money and goods, but also ideas. The sheer explosion of two-way trade cannot leave the two cultures across the Pacific intact. Over time a fusion will take place. When such fusion is perceived by the American body politic as a positive development in reinvigorating American society, the consensus, for example in favor of a continuing strong U.S. military presence as a stabilizing factor, will grow. It is evident that such fusion has already begun, with beneficial effects, especially for regional security.

The Asia-Pacific: Regional Security

It is not an accident that a region that has experienced some of the greatest wars of the twentieth century is now the most peaceful. There must be deeper forces behind this. Some have been touched on earlier in this article. Others may be hard to substantiate, but they deserve consideration. For example, one reason could be the decoupling of East Asian security from European concerns. The two "hot wars" fought in East Asia, Korea, and Vietnam were fundamentally "undertaken in large part because of a perceived linkage to European security."[14] Facile explanations also have to be questioned. U.S. military superiority in the region cannot be the only explanation (although it is undoubtedly important). If military superiority is critical, NATO should have prevented the crisis in Bosnia.

The Asia-Pacific region is developing a unique "corporate culture" on regional security: an unusual blend of East and West. It combines both Western concepts (for example, of national sovereignty as well as regional organization) and Eastern attitudes on managing differences. The best current working model is found in Southeast Asia.

Just like Europe, the continent of Asia has its own Balkans, which are also tucked away in its southeast corner. In size and diversity, however, Southeast Asia far exceeds the Balkans. It has more than 450 million people, which is ten times the population of the Balkans. In both ethnic and religious terms it is far more diverse: Islam, Christianity, Buddhism (two schools), Hinduism, Taoism, and Confucianism coexist. And, as recently as ten years ago, Southeast Asia elicited far greater pessimism than the Balkans. In 1984 the guns had been silent in Europe since World War II, but Southeast Asia had experienced communist insurgencies and more deaths during the Cold War than anywhere else.

Until as recently as 1965 the prospects for Southeast Asia looked bleak. Indonesia had experienced instability and economic decline under Sukarno; *confrontasi* against Malaysia and Singapore was continuing; Sabah was disputed by the Philippines and Malaysia; Singapore had experienced a problematic and painful merger with Malaysia; and communist insurgencies were rife in the region. All of these countries believed that the tide of history was with them. Hence the conventional wisdom, less than thirty years ago, was that Southeast Asian states would "fall like dominoes" to communism. Thus Southeast Asia should be wary of excessive optimism.

So how has Southeast Asia become the most successful part of the Third World? It is now experiencing a peace that is the envy of most of the world. And, in what is perhaps the greatest irony, the guns in the Balkans of Asia are quiet while the sound of gunfire in the Balkans of Europe suggests that it is Europe, rather than Asia, that is experiencing a "back to the future."

Southeast Asia has used several elements of the "corporate culture" for regional security. The first is the deeply rooted Asian tradition (symbolically represented by visitors taking off their shoes before entering someone's home) of respecting the household and recognizing that one enters as a guest. Hence, virtually every Asian society endorses the principle of noninterference in internal affairs. This is an old adage that also has its roots in Europe. But with the rise of universalistic assumptions in Western societies, this principle has been eroded.

In much of Europe and North America, it is considered "legitimate" to intervene in the internal affairs of a state when certain universal principles are violated, especially human rights. In North America or a Europe exhausted by war, this leads to no conflicts. But as the experience of South Asia demonstrates, commenting on internal affairs can lead to conflict in less developed states. One essential reason why no war has broken out among ASEAN states for more than twenty-five years is precisely that they adhere to the principle of noninterference in internal affairs.

ASEAN has been heavily criticized for remaining silent on East Timor. If most Asian countries do not comment on each other's domestic activities, it is probably because they believe in the old Christian adage, "Let him who has not sinned cast the first stone." All our societies are imperfect, but if we are all progressing toward a better state of affairs, why rock the boat? There is a lot of wisdom in the decision, for example, of Japan to exercise restraint in commenting on China. This supposedly "immoral" stand could in the long run save millions of lives by preventing conflict.

A second element is the Asian way of dealing with difficult relations. Apart from the propaganda crossing the ideological divide between North and South Korea (and to a lesser extent between China and Taiwan), it is striking how few East Asian nations engage in "shouting matches" with each other. "Face" is important, and conflict can break out when it is lost, such as when Vietnam humiliated China by invading Kampuchea in defiance of explicit Chinese warnings. Vietnamese diplomats have confessed in private that it had gone against two thousand years of collected wisdom in snubbing China so openly.

But Asians also accept hierarchy. When this is not violated, peace can reign. The fascination of Sino-Japanese relations is in deciding who should view whom as number one. Economically, Japan is far ahead, but in political and military terms China carries more weight. Japan is more stable than China in the short term, and China needs Japanese economic aid and investment. But Japan needs China's market, as well as social stability in China. While Japan's culture is derived from China, Japan carries more weight in the international hierarchy.

So who determines who is number one? There will be no explicit statements or understandings, but it is significant that the Japanese emperor chose to visit China in 1992, at a time when Beijing was still relatively isolated internationally. This was an unusually generous gesture on the part of Japan and may have bought a decade or two of stability for their relations. Symbolic gestures are important in Asia.

These elements indicate the different dynamics operating in the Atlantic and the Pacific. The Atlantic believes in building strong institutions: NATO, the EU, and the OSCE are the strongest in their field. Together they ensure that none of the members are directly threatened by a military invasion. But in an era when invasions are virtually inconceivable outside the usual "tinderbox" regions (for example, the Middle East and South Asia), these powerful institutions seem powerless either to defend their members from nontraditional sources of insecurity (such as rising immigrants and terrorism) or to prevent nearby conflicts (such as Algeria and Bosnia).

The Pacific has no comparable institutions but is creating networks instead. These are inclusive rather than exclusive, but, even more unusual (and this goes against the conventional wisdom in many European textbooks on international relations), their formation is driven not by the major powers, but by the middle or small powers (especially ASEAN countries). None of the recent regional initiatives were either conceived or built upon in the major capitals.

The annual July gathering of ASEAN foreign ministers was originally confined to the six member-states. Gradually others applied to attend: the European Community (1972), Australia (1974), New Zealand (1975), Japan (1977), Canada (1977), the United States (1977), and Korea (1991). There were no heavy agendas, formal communiqués, or attempts to create Helsinki-type "baskets." Instead, ASEAN emphasized personal contacts and trust building.

These July meetings paved the way for the creation of two larger region-wide institutions: APEC and the ARF. When APEC was first suggested by Australia, the United States demurred. When the rest of the region agreed to proceed without it, Washington decided to join. Initially the United States was an unenthusiastic participant, but when

Malaysia suggested establishing an East Asian Economic Caucus (EAEC), Washington decided that the best way to fight the EAEC was to strengthen APEC. Hence the United States offered to host the first APEC leaders' meeting in Seattle in November 1993 — surely the most powerful gathering of leaders in the world (if judged by the portion of the world's GNP and population represented at the meeting). Now these APEC leaders' meetings are becoming an annual event, and virtually out of nowhere a powerful institution has been established. Its quick and surefooted arrival only makes sense when viewed against the larger dynamic working in the region.

The ARF was launched in Bangkok in July 1994. Japan originally suggested it, but nothing came of it. It did become a reality, however, when ASEAN adopted the idea. After attending several ASEAN meetings, the major powers had confidence in ASEAN's ability to be an impartial but effective leader of the process. Viewed from the inside, the process seems chaotic. But viewed from the outside, it seems amazing how quickly and firmly the ARF has been established. There will eventually be an ARF summit.

APEC and the ARF are unique, because the culture that guides both institutions is a blend of East and West. The rules of procedure are Western; English is the only language spoken at meetings of officials; golf, a game with Scottish origins, is the one game they all play; but the behavioral culture within the organization is heavily influenced by Asia. Direct confrontation is avoided — "face" must not be lost. Everybody must feel "comfortable." And in both cases diversity makes them stronger. The presence of culturally diverse but comfortable "pairs" such as Australia and Indonesia, Canada and Korea, Japan and Thailand, the United States and ASEAN, and China and Malaysia, to name a few, gives the Asia-Pacific region its uniqueness.

Both APEC and the ARF, of course, are fragile new institutions. If they collapse within a year or two, or even within a decade, many assumptions about the future course of the Asia-Pacific will have been proved wrong. I have to submit my thesis to such empirical verification.

But there is good reason for confidence. APEC can only move as fast as its chairman can drive it. It has no EU-type bureaucracy to carry it.

Under the leadership of U.S. President Bill Clinton, it is not surprising that the Seattle meeting succeeded. The chairmanship, however, could not have been passed to a more different actor: Indonesian President Suharto, a quintessential Javanese leader. Yet the Bogor meeting, which he chaired, proved even more successful than the Seattle meeting, especially in setting a definite timetable for moving toward freer trade in the Asia-Pacific region.

The next APEC summit will be in Japan, which has already expressed reservations about the rapid pace of trade liberalization with APEC. Some feel that Japanese bureaucrats will be inclined to slow the progress of APEC. But Japanese leaders and thinkers are also aware that the results of the summit in Japan will be measured against the two preceding summits in the United States and Indonesia and the two succeeding summits in the Philippines and Canada. If Japan's contribution to APEC suffers in such comparison, Japan's claim to international leadership will also have been dented. As the date for the Osaka summit in November 1995 approaches, Japan will be under pressure to deliver results.

If APEC can be safely passed from one end of the cultural spectrum of the Asia-Pacific to the other without any mishap, it suggests that institutions such as APEC and the ARF are riding on a larger, more powerful underlying dynamic, which is what I call the "Pacific impulse."

Neither the Pacific nor the Atlantic impulse, however, is geographically bound. There is no reason why Europe cannot link itself closely to East Asia, as North America is doing. The recent decision by the European Union to launch an "Asia Policy" was a welcome move. If both North America and Europe were to develop the Pacific impulse, we might actually enjoy fifty more years not just of relative peace across most parts of the globe, but also a rising tide of prosperity. The opportunities are enormous.

SEVEN PARADOXES ON
ASIA-PACIFIC SECURITY

When the center of gravity of the world's economy shifts to the Asia-Pacific in the twenty-first century, the accompanying geopolitical shifts will be equally significant. The three major powers of the region (and perhaps also the world) will be the United States, China, and Japan. How they interact will determine the future of the region and also profoundly affect the rest of the world. A paradoxical Arab proverb warns of the dangers of making predictions: "He who speaks about the future lies even when he tells the truth." This paradox inspired me to make an effort to look at likely outcomes in the Asia-Pacific from a different perspective. I tried to see whether thinking in paradoxes might give us a clearer view of the future of the Asia-Pacific than straight-line projections. I came up with seven paradoxes when I was asked to address the Europe Asia Forum in February 1998.

The seven paradoxes, however, have become six. The seventh paradox has been resolved: the United States has lifted its opposition to China's entry into the WTO and has passed legislation to enable China's entry. The other six remain valid.

The greatest paradox about the region is actually not mentioned in this essay. It is mentioned in the preceding one: that the one region in the world that is experiencing the greatest shifts of power seen in the history of man also remains one of the most peaceful regions in the world. It could replace the previous paradox no. 7.

I do not know how or why I have become a lover of paradoxes. It could have been because of my contact with Heraclitus during my studies in philosophy. But I do know that paradoxes remain an excellent instrument for understanding new realities as we move into an era of unprecedented change and turbulence. The most lasting bridges built by engineers are

those that have built-in flexibility to absorb varying levels of stress.
Similarly, our minds must become ever more flexible if we are to understand
new realities. The search for and grasp of paradoxes facilitates flexible
thinking, which will help us to absorb the stress of the many new paradoxes
that will be born in the years to come.

WE ARE LIVING IN TIMES OF GREAT CHANGE, change on a scale
that has probably never before been seen in the history of man. For
the first time the Pacific Ocean will become the center of world history (just like the Atlantic or the Mediterranean were in the nineteenth and twentieth centuries). The three largest economies in the
world in the twenty-first century will be the United States, China, and
Japan. Therefore, how these three powers interact will inevitably
determine the course of the region's and possibly even the world's
history, although I say this with some trepidation in a room full of
Europeans.

This triangular relationship will be rich and complex. It will be difficult to capture in linear statements. Hence I have decided to present
seven paradoxes, in the hope that they will bring out the complexity
and lead us to be less surprised in the coming months and years.

**Paradox 1: In the Asia-Pacific change means the preservation of the
status quo.**
The first paradox is that during this period of great change the status
quo in the Asia-Pacific is peace. What we have today may be a freak of
history. We see the emergence of a new great power (China) but with
no immediate hint of conflict. The region today is not preparing for
war. It is preparing for prosperity — that is the mood and tone of the
region. The economic difficulties have only further reinforced the
point that economic, not political, issues hold center stage for now.

The value of status quo was shown when we had a crisis in March
1996. In reaction to perceived efforts by Taiwan to flirt with the idea of
independence, China conducted missile tests in the Taiwan Strait. The
United States responded by dispatching aircraft carriers. There was
tension in the air.

But this crisis may have been good for the region. The Chinese word for "crisis" is a combination of two characters: "danger" and "opportunity." We faced a danger then, but we also saw a new opportunity because it alerted key minds in Washington, Tokyo, and Beijing to the importance of preserving the status quo. A new consensus emerged in the region: "Let sleeping dogs lie." This is why we have not had any major geopolitical crisis in East Asia since March 1996 despite phenomenal historical change in our region.

Paradox 2: Japan is China's historical rival, but China needs a strong Japan.

The second paradox is that China has a strong vested interest in the two other powers staying together in an alliance. Last year China was very critical of the U.S.-Japan defense alliance, especially of the possibility of its extension to Taiwan. Quite a campaign was launched against this alliance. Certainly the extension of the U.S.-Japan defense alliance to cover Taiwan would be unacceptable to China. The reason is history. Logically, therefore, it would appear that China would be better off with a breakup of the U.S.-Japan alliance, because that would end an apparent two-against-one situation.

Paradoxically, however, it is in China's real interest to see the U.S.-Japan defense alliance continue, because if it breaks up — and Japan has to defend itself alone — Japan would surely contemplate a nuclear option. It serves neither the interest of China nor even the United States to push Japan into that nuclear corner. Hence China should see its interest in the continuation of the alliance — even though with the end of the Cold War the focus of alliance cannot be the Soviet Union, and it could become an alliance to defend Japan against China.

Paradox 3: China and Japan have been linked in many ways throughout history, but China may soon be more culturally akin to the United States than to Japan.

The continuation of the U.S.-Japan defense alliance does not mean that the United States will always remain closer to Japan than to China. The third paradox is that despite the long history of engagement between Japan and the United States, and the similarity of their economic and political systems — both are liberal democracies — we should not be surprised if the cultural comfort is greater between China and the United States than between Japan and the United States.

Having said that, let me hasten to add that this is a controversial point. It seems rather bold to suggest that an ostensibly communist society such as China could develop greater cultural comfort with an open society such as the United States than Japan could. But having observed Chinese and Japanese students in the United States, my sense is that Chinese students integrate better into U.S. culture than Japanese students do. One of Japan's real strengths is its social cohesion (it is possibly the most socially cohesive society in the world) and its cultural uniqueness. The unique Japanese tribe is an asset to mankind.

China, relatively speaking, is a somewhat more open society than Japan. Indeed, in one of its most glorious eras — during the Tang dynasty — it was open and cosmopolitan. As China becomes more prosperous in the twenty-first century it may well emulate the Tang dynasty. If it does, we could see the return of a cosmopolitan society. Hence you could have a paradoxical situation with the United States and Japan having a defense treaty alliance but, culturally, China and the United States becoming closer.

Paradox 4: U.S. benevolence, and its informal style of communication, may bring China and Japan closer to each other than ever before in their long history.

The fourth paradox is that while in the U.S.-Japan-China alliance we have two Asian societies (Japan and China) and one Western society, each of the two Asian societies feels more comfortable relating to the Western partner — the United States — than to the other Asian partner.

Historically Japan and China have lived together for millennia. The United States is the new kid on the block. It is only two hundred years old, and it has been in Asia just over one hundred years. Hence the relations of Japan and China with the United States are not heavily burdened with history. The United States is also a unique great power, probably the most benevolent great power ever seen in the history of man. Apart from its colonization of the Philippines and Cuba, it has had in general no expansionist designs. Indeed, the Asia-Pacific region will be far worse off if the United States leaves than if it stays.

In addition to this benevolence, the United States provides an open Western form of communication, which is more effective than the polite Asian methods, where you never say what you really think. The Seattle APEC leaders' meeting demonstrated the American genius for informality.

Paradox 5: East Asian alliances will help to retain U.S. engagement in the Asia-Pacific.

The fifth paradox is that if we agree that it is in the best interest of China and Japan (and indeed of all East Asian countries) to see the United States continue its presence in the region, then the best way of assuring that it will is for East Asian countries to draw closer to each other.

We saw the value of East Asian cooperation in the early 1990s. Initially the United States was skeptical of APEC (a multilateral arrangement). However, after Malaysia proposed the East Asian Economic Caucus (EAEC), interest in APEC increased because it was seen as a counter to the EAEC. Similarly, it was good that there was a historic meeting in Kuala Lumpur in December 1997 between ASEAN, China, Japan, and Korea. Eventually, if all goes well, the combined GNP of East Asia will become larger than that of North America and Europe combined. East Asian closeness will strengthen the hand of those who argue that the United States should remain engaged and not withdraw from East Asia. This will help to contain isolationism or unilateral tendencies in the United States. The United States is a unique great power as it has the most divided decision-making mechanism at the highest levels. East Asia can stimulate continued U.S. engagement not by drifting apart but by drifting together.

Paradox 6: Contradiction and division in the U.S. government benefit Asia.

The sixth paradox is that while this divided decision-making process of the United States is a source of anxiety or annoyance to many Asian countries, it actually benefits Asia as much as it does the United States. One example: China. Despite the United States' stated adherence to a one-China policy, Congress passed the Taiwan Relations Act, which contradicts the one-China policy. However, despite their annoyance, East Asian countries should welcome the checks and balances of the U.S. system because the net result — usually — is a benevolent U.S. policy.

The main reason why Americans operate with a light touch overseas is that the administration does not have all the power in its hands. Just imagine how the United States would behave if President Clinton had as much power as Stalin. Therefore Asians should tolerate the annual debate on MFN renewal, human rights, and trade imbalances, because they are part of the noise that goes with the U.S. system. Our challenge is to educate decision makers to restrain themselves in congressional debates.

Paradox 7: The United States needs China in the WTO but opposes its entry.
The seventh paradox is that even though it is the United States that is placing the greatest obstacles in the path of early Chinese membership of the WTO (and I realize this is a controversial statement), it is actually more in the United States' than in China's interest to see a faster Chinese membership in the WTO. The emergence of China as a major economy cannot be stopped. It will become larger and larger. The sooner it plays by international rules, the better it will be for the United States and the international community. Of course, if the United States wants to educate China on how to be a good citizen and play by WTO rules, then it should set an example by reexamining the WTO's inconsistent legislations, such as the Helms-Burton Act, the D'Amato Act, and so on. Hence, if the United States really studied what was in its long-term interests, it should be doing the exact opposite of what it is doing with China and the WTO and push for early rather than late entry of China into the WTO.

In conclusion, let me hope that I have not confused you about the geopolitical picture of this region with my seven paradoxes. However, as someone who has a ringside seat in the arena of the greatest and the most rapid change in the history of man, I feel that it is my duty to alert you to these developments. My final parting paradox is this: it will not be surprising if there are surprising developments in our region.

GLOBAL CONCERNS

UN: SUNRISE OR SUNSET ORGANIZATION IN THE TWENTY-FIRST CENTURY?

One quirk in my diplomatic career has been that I have been posted as ambassador to the UN not once, but twice. My Hindu ancestors would surely believe that this was fate: I was born on United Nations Day.

As a result, I have developed a deep empathy and affection for the UN. Among the hardheaded strategic thinkers, it is considered softheaded to be a defender of the UN. The UN therefore needs a hardheaded defense. This is what this essay, first published in fall 2000, tries to provide.

In writing this I had no choice but to deal squarely with the biggest threat faced by the UN: the attitude of the world's only superpower. The great paradox here is that a strong UN serves, rather than hurts, larger American interests. Unfortunately, few American intellectuals have had the interest or the courage to defend the UN. Hence this essay. For the sake of completeness I have also included a brief op-ed article that I published in the Wall Street Journal *in October 1986 (see page 180).*

The events of 11 September 2001 have completely changed the political landscape for the UN, especially vis-à-vis the only superpower. As Francis Fukuyama wrote in an essay in Financial Times *on 15 September 2001, "The U.S. is likely to emerge from the attacks a different country, more unified, less self-absorbed, and much more in need of the help of its friends to carry out what will become a new national project of defeating terrorism. And it may also become a more ordinary country in the sense of having concrete interests and real vulnerabilities, rather than thinking itself unilaterally able to define the nature of the world it lives in." If Fukuyama's prediction comes true, the nature of the U.S.–UN relationship will also change.*

THE SIMPLE BUT STARTLING PARADOX ABOUT THE UN is that at a historical moment when the need for the UN has never been greater, it still faces a real vulnerability: the danger of going the way of its predecessor, the League of Nations. This is not a likely development, but it remains very much in the realm of possibility.

An equally sad reality is that even if the UN survives, it may survive through much of this century only in its present crippled form: accepted as part of the international furniture but hobbled carefully so that it cannot take a major role. The least likely possibility for the UN is that it will emerge as a dynamic multilateral institution whose historical moment has finally arrived; that is, a body equipped to cope with the new interdependent and interconnected world generated by globalization. To understand how and why this historical moment has arrived, we should all read in full the bold report that the secretary-general has prepared for the Millennium Summit. This report clearly outlines the tasks facing the "world's peoples" in the twenty-first century and suggests how the UN can be a more useful instrument for tackling them. The analysis is clear and sobering. After reading it, it is hard to believe that the UN could have been put into such a precarious state.

The purpose of this article is to explain how the UN arrived at its present quandary. Too much of the writing on the UN, even by its vociferous American critics, avoids dealing with the real issues at stake. This article will try to provide new perspectives on the reasons for the UN's perceived failures. Perhaps in the course of this analysis some suggestions might emerge on how to revitalize the UN. Let me confess that even though the prospects for this happening do look bleak at this stage, the ceremonies of the Millennium Summit in September 2000 may give a different public impression.

The big silent "conspiracy" that has surrounded the UN since its creation is a tacit understanding among all major powers, including both the Soviet Union and the United States during the Cold War, that they are better off with a weaker UN. Each would have preferred a pliable UN but their conflicting wishes canceled each other out. Hence, for most of its existence, the UN has been crippled not by accident but by design.

A Moment of Vulnerability

The ostensible crisis that the UN faces today is financial. The United States, the largest contributor, has held back payments from the days of the Reagan administration, leading to arrears of U.S.$1.7 billion. In an apparent effort to resolve this problem, the Senate passed the Helms-Biden Act in late 1999, which, *inter alia*, offered to pay up to U.S.$926 million of these arrears to all UN organizations on condition that the U.S. contributions to the regular and peacekeeping budgets were reduced to 22 percent and 25 percent, respectively, from the previous agreed assessments of 25 percent 31 percent.[2]

These demands are outrageous. At the moment of the greatest economic prosperity that the United States has enjoyed (with its share of the global GNP growing to around 27 percent), the United States is asking other nations to effectively subsidize its share of contributions to the UN. What makes this doubly outrageous is that the United States is one of the main beneficiaries of the UN system, both financially and in other terms.[3] The only saving grace here is that responsible American officials admit, in private, that these demands are excessive.

It would be foolish of me to make any prediction on how this latest UN financial crisis will be resolved. Clearly it would serve the UN's long-term interests to have the problem solved once and for all. Dynamic American diplomacy, under the leadership of U.S. permanent representative to the UN, Ambassador Richard Holbrooke, could lead to the squaring of the circle: where the most rich ask the less rich to pay more. But it could just as well fail, for the simple reason that it is an incredibly difficult and complex task to devise a new scale of assessments that will be considered fair by the remaining 187 UN member states when the richest state of the world is made to pay less.

The Real Issue: Power

Whatever the outcome of this current financial crisis, it will not resolve the real factors leading to the crippling of the UN: considerations of power. Ever since the activist days of Dag Hammarskjold, the last UN secretary-general to attempt to forge a new role for the UN both as a conscience and as an independent international actor, the major powers have agreed that, whatever their differences, they are all better off with a less independent and more compliant UN. Hence, for the past few decades, the UN has been relegated to a peripheral role in international affairs. The UN was clearly told to stay clear of many important and vital international issues (such as the Vietnam War, the Middle East peace process [after some initial involvement]), even though the UN Charter clearly mandates the UN Security Council with "the primary responsibility for international peace and security."

A quick qualification. The UN, though hobbled, has not been completely passive over the past few decades. Shrewd secretaries-general have carefully created positive roles for the UN in areas that complemented the interests of the major powers. The UN has done sterling work in peacekeeping, fully deserving of the Nobel Peace Prize it won in this area. The Cuban missile crisis was partially resolved under UN auspices. The Gulf War success could not have been accomplished without the UN umbrella. Taking advantage of the end of the Cold War, Javier Perez de Cuellar was able to bring solutions to long-simmering conflicts, as in El Salvador, the Iran-Iraq war, Namibia, and Mozambique. A key aide, Gianni Picco, at some risk to his own life, helped to solve the Lebanese hostage crisis. And he was not the only UN staff member to risk his life to save American citizens. Much sterling work has been done in humanitarian areas. In short, much good work has been done over the years by the UN, much of it unrecognized and unrewarded. The honest truth is that the UN has never been given full credit for its many contributions.

Yet, despite this, when the history of the twentieth century is written, the UN will at best merit a few footnotes.[4] Most historians will not portray it as a central actor of the century. For this to change in the twenty-first century, the major powers will have to decide that it is in their national interest to see a stronger, rather than weaker, UN. None are close to making such a decision.

In the past two decades the United States has done more damage to the UN than any other power. Much of it was the result of an irrational and angry reaction to the Third World domination of the agenda of the UN General Assembly and other multilateral fora in the 1970s and early 1980s. But when the Third World domination ended, the U.S. attacks against the UN continued, often in an incoherent form. As Gene Lyons notes, "The United States has been seemingly obsessed with reforming UN management and dealing with overloaded bureaucracies, overlapping programs, and unaudited finances — not without reason but without equally expounding on where the world is going and how the UN fits in."[5] The recent history of UN bashing by the United States is so well known that it need not be repeated here.

But the United States also provides, paradoxically, the last great hope for the UN. In the effectively unipolar world that we live in in the early twenty-first century, decisions made in Washington, D.C., are the most crucial. At present no senior American figure believes that the strengthening of the UN serves vital American interests. Only this can explain why the UN has been allowed to be made into a political football in Washington, used to bolster other interests (as, for instance, Congressman Chris Smith's maneuvers to delay a resolution of UN financing by linking it to the abortion issue).

A case can be made, if a brave senior American figure is prepared to stand up to the winds of political correctness, that the time has come for a radical rethinking of American strategy toward the UN. As Gene Lyons notes, "The world has changed, but US relations with the UN are still stuck in the same rut."[6] For an open society, American thinking, especially on international issues, easily flows into a rut. The UN is no exception.

Globalization

What makes the absence of new thinking on the UN even more surprising is that the case for a stronger UN is bizarrely simple as well as obvious. American technology has changed the world. Distance has disappeared, as the world has shrunk to a global village, and every village needs a village council. The UN represents the only real village council we have. There is no other.

Daily, the forces of globalization are generating greater and greater interdependence. Actions in one corner of the world can affect a distant corner relatively quickly. Most people living outside the United States can feel and understand the impact of globalization: they feel a loss of autonomy each day. Most Americans do not feel this, or not yet. They live in one of the most powerful countries ever to have existed in the history of man. Sheer power and two huge oceans make Americans unaware of how the world is changing. The great paradox here is that the world's most open society is among the worst informed on the inevitable impact of global changes. A tidal wave of change is already on its way to American shores. The current overwhelming power and geographic isolation is at best a temporary dam holding back the inevitable impact of globalization on American society. And when the dam is breached Americans will regret not having used the window of opportunity available to them (when they were clearly and overwhelmingly powerful relative to the rest of the world) to strengthen the UN to help deal with the small interdependent world emerging. Of course many Americans firmly believe that they will be the most powerful forever. History teaches us otherwise.

Perhaps another simple analogy will help to explain to Americans why an effective UN serves American interests. Americans, like anyone else, understand the need for traffic rules. Without such rules highways and interchanges could not function. With globalization new global highways are being opened daily, literally and metaphorically. The traffic of people, money, ideas, goods, and so forth around the world is going to increase at an exponential pace. What will happen if we destroy or weaken the only organization (or, more accurately, the UN family of organizations) capable of providing a viable setting for the formulation of larger global rules?

So far, a few Americans have begun seeing the impact of interdependence in a few areas. They now understand that a new Ebola virus in Africa can reach American shores overnight. Viruses do not need passports. They do not respect borders. Neither do environmental disasters. Americans have not experienced a Chernobyl yet, but they are beginning to understand that climate change can also affect them. In the world of finance, where the United States now appears to reign supreme, the Asian financial crisis proved that a crisis emerging in a distant Southeast Asian country, Thailand, could eventually ripple into American stock markets via Korea, Russia, and Brazil. This was a healthy scare. It has made senior American finance officials more aware of global interdependence than their colleagues in other areas. It would be a pity if similar scares and disasters are necessary to open the eyes of other American officials.

It is vital to stress here that no one can foretell the future in specific terms. We all know that technology will change the future of the globe; more so the explosive and exponential growth of new technology that we are experiencing now. Someone once said that while we cannot tell the future, we can predict the level of floods in the Ganges River if we know how much snow fell in the Himalayas the preceding winter. The two are inextricably linked. Today we know that the "heavy snowfall" of new technology has descended upon the globe. The floods of change are coming. This much we can be certain about. It is strange therefore not to begin preparing for it.

The UN's Role

But what can the UN do to help cope with the impending floods? How can a fragile, much-ravaged institution be a leader in global change? It has stumbled in crises in small countries such as Rwanda and Bosnia. How can the UN realistically take on major global burdens? These are fair questions.

To respond to them fairly, some conceptual clarity is needed. Most laymen see the UN system as one institution. It is actually a family of institutions. Some are completely independent, such as the International Labor Organization (ILO), the World Health Organization (WHO), and so on. Some are related and dependent, such as the United Nations Development Programme (UNDP) and the United Nations International Children's Emergency Fund (UNICEF). But at the core, there are three principal organs that play critically different roles: the UN Security Council, the UN General Assembly, and the UN Secretariat.

The Security Council represents the aristocracy. Within it, the permanent five (United States, Russia, China, U.K., and France) exercise tremendous powers, both formally and informally. As the UN Charter confers upon the Security Council "primary responsibility for peace and security," it is the only body that authoritatively deals with vital issues of war and peace. Decisions of the council, taken by 15 members, are binding on all 188 member states.

The UN General Assembly represents the masses. All 188 member states, in an affirmation of sovereign equality, have an equal vote in the General Assembly. But the decisions of the assembly are not binding, even though most are adopted by consensus. At best, they are recommendations. Finally, the UN Secretariat. It is technically only the implementing arm of the UN. It is accountable to the assembly in theory, but in practice it pays greater heed to the views of the council (which has a decisive say in the appointment of the secretary-general). The secretary-general does have a capacity to launch independent initiatives and act as a moral force. The personal prestige and stature of the individual secretary-general does matter.

Each of these units will therefore make different contributions to the new role that the UN will play in an increasingly interdependent world. A few examples may help to clarify the picture. First, *norm setting* will become an increasingly important role for the UN. As the world changes, new norms will have to be created both for the multilateral architecture as well as multilateral processes of the world. The creation of norms, if they are to be accepted in practice, has to be a consensual exercise (which almost by definition makes it a painful exercise). The conversion of these norms into binding legal obligations has to be done in the UN. All new global norms — in the law of the sea, in environmental conventions, in land mines, in the International Criminal Court — have been created either under the aegis of the UN General Assembly or in global conferences that are offshoots of the General Assembly (for example, the Rio, Cairo, Copenhagen, and Beijing summits). Without this assembly (or an equivalent), the world would be paralyzed with its old norms. Indeed the global advances in respect for human rights have only been made possible because of their legitimization by UN processes.

Second, to deal with specific crises that emerge from time to time and engage global attention (for example, East Timor, Kosovo, and Sierra Leone), the world has to agree on the process of *burden sharing*.

Some disputes are now resolved primarily outside the UN (for example, Kosovo). But eventually they have to be brought under the UN umbrella to gain international legitimacy. Not all countries can get involved in all disputes. Geography, political interests, treaty relationships, and cultural links help determine which countries will play the lead in solving which conflict. Both history and geography, as well as strong U.S. prodding, for example, led to Australia's leadership role in East Timor. But it could not have intervened on its own without the legitimizing role of the Security Council and the participation of other regional countries. Each new peacekeeping operation (PKO) that is created also means that the world as a whole will take responsibility for a specific problem, rather than a region. Until the UN Security Council got involved, the Economic Community of West African States Cease-Fire Monitoring Group (ECOMOG) had to pay the bills for Sierra Leone. But when the UN took over, all 188 countries had to foot the bill. All these decisions can be made only by the UN Security Council.

The secretary-general for his part can provide both moral and intellectual leadership. It is surely an amazing fact that on this planet of six billion human beings only one human being appears to symbolize the collective interests of all humanity combined. When he speaks, therefore, he can draw global attention to global concerns in a way that virtually no one else can. The current secretary-general, Mr. Kofi Annan, has been relatively bold in suggesting new ideas. In response to the crises in Bosnia, Rwanda, and Kosovo, he has suggested, for example, that the international community has a duty to undertake humanitarian intervention within sovereign states if massive human rights violations occur. This is a bold idea. No other global leader has had the courage to make this case.

These three examples help to explain the constructive role the UN can play in coping with the new world. None of these functions can be easily performed by others. The G-7 (now G-8) leaders, for example, sometimes make crucial decisions on key global issues. They can move financial markets with their decisions (for instance, the Plaza Accords). But, in the real world, they have no means to either impose their views on other nation-states (without the legal authority of the

Security Council) or have them viewed as legitimate by the international community (without the General Assembly's endorsement). Within any modern society the rich have no authority to make decisions for the whole society. Nor can the G-7 speak on behalf of the international community. Only the UN or its secretary-general have the institutional and moral legitimacy to do so. President Clinton himself told the UN General Assembly in September 1999 that the UN was an indispensable institution.

Working with the World Population

But there is another indispensable element, which cannot be ignored in preparing the world for a new future: the wishes of the six billion people who inhabit the planet. Americans tend to make a natural assumption that what is good for the United States is naturally good for the world (perhaps an extension of the old adage that what is good for General Motors was good for the United States). But there is a great diversity of needs, interests, and aspirations among the six billion. The great challenge that the world faces is that of harmonizing and balancing the needs and interests of six billion people on a shrinking planet.

It is only natural that there should be a difference of needs and interests between the rich and the poor. The poor want economic development. By contrast, the rich have a vested interest in the status quo. Hence, for example, the United States and most other developed countries have a vital interest in preventing the spread of weapons of mass destruction, especially the new-generation chemical and biological weapons. Conventions to restrict their development have been negotiated and adopted through the General Assembly process, clumsy and slow though this may be. But the only real way to prevent their proliferation is by creating a global consensus, in which all the countries have a common stake in global peace and prosperity. To have such a stake, each society — no matter how rich or poor, small or big — must feel that it is a stakeholder in a global community.

Effective participation in UN processes converts all nations into stakeholders. Both psychologically and materially, all nations must feel that they have a say in the management of the globe. Just as democracy elicits the commitment of the citizen to respect the results of the elections and the subsequent decisions of the elected government, a vote in the UN delivers a similar commitment from the nation-states. Neither nationally nor internationally do these processes work perfectly. But the crucial role that the UN plays in making stakeholders out of each nation is neither well understood nor appreciated.

As the world's largest economy and with the greatest range of global interests, the United States is indeed the single biggest beneficiary of the stabilizing role that the UN plays. Ed Luck has stated succinctly several times that the United States has a fundamental interest in the United Nations as an institution, because it has an unquestionable stake in international law, order, and stability. However imperfectly the UN performs this function, the world body is, on balance, a net contributor to a more orderly, predictable, norm-abiding, and hence stable world.

This statement is simple and commonsensical. Yet few Americans, especially politicians, are able to grasp it or see it. The reason is simple. They have been blinded by stories from the media on how "anti-American" the UN General Assembly has become, especially during the 1970s. In that decade there was a close alliance between the Arabs and the Africans to work together to secure strong majorities against apartheid rule in South Africa and Israeli occupation of Arab lands. The United States was often implicitly and explicitly criticized in these resolutions. It then became fashionable for Americans to rail against "the tyranny of the majority" in the General Assembly. This in turn sparked a decade of UN-bashing in the U.S. Congress, creating more and more absurd conditions for the UN to fulfill before the UN could receive its legally assessed funding from the U.S. Congress.

The great paradox here that few Americans have grasped is that the demonstrated independence of the General Assembly from U.S. domination — while not serving some short-term American interests — does indeed serve long-term American interests. If the General Assembly had become perceived as a compliant American instrument, it would have lost the respect, trust, and commitment of the 5.75 billion people who live outside the United States. The more independent the General Assembly is seen to be, the greater their confidence in it — and the stronger their commitment to the larger norm-generating activities of the assembly. The greater their commitment to these norms, the more the larger American interests are served.

The failure of American policymakers (especially those in Congress) to understand this paradox has led them on a futile course of trying, to use a crude analogy, to squeeze both ends of a tube of toothpaste. If you squeeze both the top and bottom ends, no toothpaste will come out. With sufficient pressure, the tube will eventually break. The same could happen to the UN if the United States squeezes both ends (that is, to make the UN appear compliant to American interests and simultaneously try to make it an effective instrument to manage larger global interests).

Hence, instead of railing against the UN each time the General Assembly or (rarely) the Security Council demonstrates its independence of American wishes or demands, American policymakers should quietly cheer on the UN. The United States need have no real fear that without the current U.S. Congress's sword of Damocles hanging over the UN, the UN will turn fundamentally anti-American. This cannot happen for a simple reason: most of the world shares the fundamental U.S. interest in, as Ed Luck says, "international law, order and stability."

Occasionally, where these interests differ, the short-term American interests may not necessarily be in the interest of the globe or in American long-term interests. A particularly egregious example may make the point clearly. Americans believe that they have a natural right to low gasoline prices. They scream when the prices increase. Yet if the rest of the world matched American levels of per capita gasoline consumption, the world would be in deep trouble, in both the economic and environmental fields. For the long-term interests of the globe (including the United States), the international community should pressure the United States to increase its gasoline price and rationalize its consumption patterns. Of course, if anyone were to suggest this now, there would be howls of protest from Americans.

There are many other such areas where U.S. policies do not necessarily serve either global or long-term American interests. The rejection of the ratification of the Comprehensive Test Ban Treaty (CTBT) was a disaster. Even the close European allies of the United States said so. So too potentially is the American effort to unilaterally walk away from the Antiballistic Missile (ABM) Treaty (a bilateral treaty that the UN General Assembly has endorsed as vital to multilateral arms control). If the United States, as the world's leading status quo power, walks away from treaty obligations, it is only opening the door for others to do so. The United States should have thanked, not chided, the General Assembly when it called on the United States to abide by its ABM Treaty obligations in November 1999.

Swallowing Paradoxes

American policymakers are not used to thinking in terms of paradoxes. The American worldview, which seems to be deeply rooted in old American myths, tends to see the world in black-and-white terms. Throughout their history, Americans fought well when the "enemies" that they had to cope with were clear and simple: the "scalp hunters" (Native Americans), the dark forces of slavery, the Nazi reign of terror, or the "Red Menace." The enemy had to be clear and demonized for the United States to be galvanized into action.

For a while the UN came close to being demonized, but either through luck or through hidden sources of wisdom, the UN managed to escape such demonization. It was a shrewd move by Ambassador Richard Holbrooke to invite Senator Jesse Helms to attend and address the august chambers of the UN Security Council. When Senator Helms did this, and when he persuaded Kofi Annan to take pictures with his family (and subsequently even invited Kofi Annan to address his alma mater in South Carolina), he lost the capacity to demonize the UN.

But the real challenge that American policymakers will face in dealing with the UN is that they will be denied the opportunity to characterize the UN in black-and-white terms. The American policymakers' minds will have to learn to cope with paradoxes and contradictions in trying to formulate coherent long-term strategies for the UN.

A few examples may help to explain this point. American technology is slowly but inexorably creating a global community where global interests will have to be both understood and dealt with. But the only global organization available to manage global interests is the United Nations, which, despite the preambular words of the UN Charter, does *not* defend the common global interests of mankind; rather, it acts as a clearing-house for the varied interests of 188 nation-states. The secretary-general captured this new challenge succinctly in his Millennium Report:

> Here, however, is the crux of our problem today: while the post-war multilateral system made it possible for the new globalization to emerge and flourish, globalization, in turn, has progressively rendered its designs antiquated. Simply put, our post-war institutions were built for an inter-*national* world, but we now live in a *global* world. Responding effectively to this shift is the core institutional challenge for world leaders today.[7]

It is conceivable that leaders and diplomats working to defend their national interests may end up inadvertently boosting global interests. But the record so far, especially of American diplomats in processes such as the Law of the Sea Conference, show that American diplomats find it difficult to reconcile national with global interests.

The latest fashion among American and some other Western intellectuals is to believe that when selfish government individuals have failed to protect common global concerns, the representatives of civil society and nongovernmental organizations (NGOs) can act as a better conscience of mankind. In theory this should be so. But as the battle of Seattle showed at the WTO conference, NGOs and civil society are no less prisoners of their sectoral interests. They may find it easy to seize the moral high ground, because in the American scheme of things nongovernmental representatives believe they represent the public good better than government representatives do. But, as demonstrated in Seattle, most Third World diplomats were mystified by the claims of these NGOs to speak on behalf of the six billion people when they had little understanding of or connection with their needs.

Altruism is a mask that has been worn by many in history, but the principle has been rarely implemented in practice. In real life, governments, business corporations, and nongovernmental organizations do not behave in fundamentally different ways: each seeks to defend its own interests (even if they believe that their interests best represent mankind's interests). The U.S. government may have a strong case for defending the patent interests of large pharmaceutical companies, but it would be unwise to deny that this can also effectively lead to deprivation of medicine and the loss of millions of lives. This point came through loud and clear in the UN Security Council debate on AIDS in January 2000. Similarly, Greenpeace may feel that it is doing mankind a favor by saving whales from Japanese whalers. But the list of endangered species is a long one. Why pick on Japan and not some other country? Who should make such a decision and how?

The point of all these examples is a simple one. The world is being driven inexorably into a single global community. A simple enlightened policy for the world to adopt at this stage would be to put into place — ahead of time — the right multilateral processes and institutions required to manage the world to come. But in another brilliant example of the constant folly that mankind has displayed throughout its history, the only power in the world that is truly capable of working out such a wise and enlightened policy — the United States — is doing the exact opposite: it is being driven by narrow political considerations to defend parochial over global interests. Future historians will surely be mystified that the United States is effectively imposing sunset provisions on the one sunrise organization that the world will need in the twenty-first century. But that's life!

U.S. Doesn't Bear Excessive Share Of U.N. Costs

The Wall Street Journal, October 30, 1986

The United Nations is perched on the edge of a financial cliff. On Monday, the U.S. announced that it would contribute only $100 million to the U.N. budget this year, less than half of its obligations under the U.N. Charter. In addition, the Soviet Union owes the U.N. about $242 million, a sum that represents payments that have not been made for several years running. If the two superpowers, along with some other smaller nations, fail to pay their dues, the U.N. may fall off the cliff. As in any crisis, many key points have been clouded. My fear is that the following 10 facts may never become visible.

Fact No. 1:

The U.N. has never had a deficit budget. Most organizations and indeed governments get into trouble when they borrow money in order to spend more than they earn. The member states of the U.N. have always denied it permission to borrow money.

Fact No. 2:

The U.N. budget is not out of control. In recent years, in response to pressures from major contributor states, the U.N. Secretariat has presented what are effectively zero-growth budgets. The U.N. is therefore understandably puzzled that good behavior is rewarded with financial sanctions, such as the withholding of contributions.

Fact No. 3:

The financial crisis is a result of illegal decisions made by certain members not to pay their dues. This is not the statement of a Third World state. The European Community in an official statement said that the "responsibility for the present financial crisis of the U.N. lies with all Member States that do not fulfill their financial obligations under the Charter." The EC also stressed that financial obligations are no different from other treaty obligations.

Fact No. 4:

This is not the first financial crisis the U.N. has experienced. In 1964, the deliberations of the U.N. General

Assembly had to be virtually suspended because the Soviet Union, having accumulated withholdings amounting to two years of its assessments, was technically in default. When the Soviet Union was responsible for that financial crisis, all the reporting stressed that the Soviet government was acting illegally.

Fact No. 5:

The largest contributor to the U.N.'s budget (the U.S.) is not paying more than its fair share. U.N. contributions are normally assessed as a percentage of national income, but the U.S. (as the largest contributor) enjoys a ceiling on the amount of its contributions. If it were assessed like any other member state, without special preference, it should be paying 28% or 29% rather than 25% of the U.N. budget. The U.S. is getting a subsidy of 3% to 4% from other member states.

Fact No. 6:

The U.N.'s system of taxation is regressive rather than progressive, i.e. the poorest member states already pay a much larger share of their income toward the U.N. than the richest states. As a percentage of national income, the top five contributors are Guinea-Bissau (.93%), Zambia (.45%), Congo (.44%), Sao Tome and Principe (.40%) and Democratic Yemen (.35%). If the U.S. paid the same share of national income that Guinea-Bissau did, it would be assessed $18 billion instead of a little over $200 million.

Fact No. 7:

The largest single beneficiary in financial terms from the U.N. is the U.S. The U.N. community spends approximately $800 million annually in New York City alone, giving the U.S. a 4-to-1 return ratio on its assessed contribution to the regular budget. The U.N. therefore is a net economic benefit to the U.S., strange as this may sound.

Fact No. 8:

The U.N. does not spend most of its budget on political activities. Only 10% is spent in such a manner.

Fact No. 9:

The U.N. is not a tool of Soviet diplomacy. The Soviet Union is as suspicious of the U.N. as the U.S. is. Whatever their disagreements the two superpowers fully agree that a strong and vigorous U.N., led say by an aggressive personality like the late Dag Hammarskjold, is not in the interest of either power.

Fact No. 10:

The 159 member states do not have an equal say over the management of the U.N. This is not a classless society. There are two classes of members: the five permanent member states of the Security Council — the U.S., the Soviet Union, the United Kingdom, France and China — and then the rest, the hoi polloi, including Singapore. As Inis Claude said in his classic study of international organizations, "Swords Into Plowshares":

> In its Security Council version, the veto is a
> weighting device, an acknowledgment of the
> inequality of states and a means of giving effect
> to the principle that the most powerful and
> important states should have special status in
> international organisations. It spells special
> privilege for the big five.

In any organization, rights go with duties, privileges go hand in hand with obligations. In the U.N., the five permanent member states enjoy special privileges — but no special obligations, not even the obligation to meet their financial payments. In fact, four out of the five (including the Soviet Union and the U.S.) have in the past contributed to the illegal process of withholding contributions.

These ten facts do not tell the whole story. The U.N. Secretariat's management defects and the irresponsible behavior of some of the U.N.'s legislative bodies have been well documented. Many of these criticisms are valid. But, is the world better off without a U.N.?

In this shrinking world, the need for a U.N. has never been greater. The global village needs a village council. If we had to start over again, could we do any better than the framers of the U.N. Charter did in 1945? Would the Soviet Union and the U.S. retain the privileges they enjoy under the present charter? Ironically, after pressuring for reform for several years, the developed slates are about to pull the plug at a time when the impetus toward reform has clearly begun. Perhaps the U.N. should be given some breathing room to complete the process of reform.

BRIDGING THE DIVIDE:
THE SINGAPORE EXPERIENCE

In the past few decades, the dominant story about Third World countries is a litany of their failures. Much less has been written about their successes, which, though significant, have been tragically few. The second volume of Mr. Lee Kuan Yew's memoirs fills an important gap in development studies: in it he explains the complex policies that led to Singapore's success.

As Kofi Annan said, "The title of this book, From Third World to First, *expresses an aspiration of all developing countries but so far, alas, an achievement of very few. Singapore is one of those few. This account of its first years of independence written by its founding father, Lee Kuan Yew, will therefore be of great interest to people of other developing countries and to all those who are interested in their fate."*

The story of Singapore's success will, however, remain buried for a while more. The prevailing media gurus, especially those in the West, have decided that the conventional wisdom about Singapore should be "Yes, Singapore has succeeded, but . . ." And the emphasis is always on the sentences that flow after the "but," not on the bare statement that precedes it.

The tragedy here is that the Western media, with their global coverage, have suppressed a story that would be both useful and inspiring to Third World populations. My international experience has taught me that there is great interest in Singapore's story. Hence I was happy to contribute this article to the Davos World Economic Forum's new daily newspaper in January 2001.

WHEN SINGAPORE GAINED INDEPENDENCE IN 1965, its leaders cried rather than cheered. The idea that a small island city-state of two million people with no hinterland could survive in what was then a difficult and troubled region seemed manifestly absurd. The odds were always against Singapore succeeding. Remarkably, it has not only succeeded, beating the odds, it has actually become one of the most successful developing nations in the world.

Beating the odds is now a challenge not just for small, vulnerable states such as Singapore but also for our planet. As we approach the end of the twentieth century, a growing concern in many minds around the globe is that we live on an overpopulated and ecologically threatened planet. In one hundred years Earth's population has trebled from 1.6 billion in 1900 to 6 billion in 2000, creating a global average of about 35 persons per square kilometer. Bangladesh, a modern metaphor for overpopulation, has 855 persons per square kilometer. However, the most crowded country in the world is Singapore, with 5,900 persons per square kilometer.

Singapore's success story is now relatively well known, despite the regular knocks it receives from some liberal Western media. But because some of these knocks have been globally transmitted, few have heard the even more interesting story of the innovative social and economic strategies that led to the success story. Singapore's innovative solutions to common economic and social problems may be worth the careful attention of those striving to bridge the growing divide in an increasingly troubled planet. It is timely for the Davos World Economic Forum to address this issue and perhaps equally timely for the *Forum News Daily* to take a peek at Singapore's story.

The economic success of Singapore is well known. Its economy has grown by more than 7 percent per annum since independence in 1965, leading to a per capita income of U.S.$29,610 (ranked ninth in the world). Some maintain that Singapore has the most efficient port, airport, airline, and civil service in the world. It also has the third largest oil-refining capability and one of the largest financial centers. Its total trade is three times the size of its GNP. The policy prescriptions created to achieve this were relatively simple: sustain a free and open economy, avoid any subsidy, welcome foreign investment, and aim for budgetary surpluses. Hard work, thrift, and the virtues of increasing worker productivity were always emphasized.

Hidden behind this economic story, however, is another story that is surprisingly little known. Societies should ultimately be judged on their ability to deliver most of their citizens' human needs: food, shelter, health, education, a clean environment, a sense of community, and a sense of purpose in life. It is in these areas that Singapore could perhaps provide recipes for success on a crowded planet, and the second volume of Mr. Lee Kuan Yew's memoirs, entitled *From Third World to First* provides rare firsthand insight into how the nation's policies were forged.

The socioeconomic policies of Singapore fit neither the capitalist nor the socialist paradigm. Instead, a healthy pragmatic spirit and an openness to innovation and experience characterize the approach of the government. Food is cheap and plentiful, because imports are encouraged from all over the world. Singapore produces no food at home, but the average worker can buy lunch for two to three U.S. dollars. Shelter is also plentiful. Ninety percent of the population lives in high-rise government-built housing that occupies only one-sixth of the island. The average dwelling space per family is above the global average. Virtually all Singaporeans live in homes they own because of a compulsory savings program (the Central Provident Fund [CPF]). A worker earning U.S.$1,000 a month (and many do earn this much) would save at least U.S.$400 every month: U.S.$200 from his salary and U.S.$200 from a matching employers' contribution. Their investment in housing has paid off, because the average flat has trebled in value over the past ten years.

The CPF scheme also enables most Singaporeans to save for medical expenses. The health system has moved away from full government subsidy to increasing copayment. However, no one who needs medical treatment is denied it, because of three-tier protection: personal savings through Medisave, a government low-cost insurance scheme through Medishield, and government assistance through Medifund. The population has become healthier every year. Infant mortality rates have fallen from 26.3 per 1,000 live births in 1965 to 3.2 per 1,000 today. Life expectancy is rising. Education is neither totally free nor compulsory, but today 90 percent of children entering school each year will complete at least ten years of education; 20 percent will complete university; 40 percent will complete polytechnic training; and 30 percent will complete vocational training. Early educational streaming ensures that different talents are recognized and developed from an early age.

The story on the environmental front is also worth studying. Long before the Green movement surfaced, the then prime minister, Lee Kuan Yew, said, "I have always believed that a blighted urban landscape, a concrete jungle, destroys the human spirit. We need the greenery of nature to lift our spirits." With careful land planning, only 49 percent of the island is used for residential, commercial, and industrial purposes. Hence half the island consists of forest reserves, water catchment areas, marshes, and other non-built up areas. It is a green island, even though the World Bank classifies the population as "one hundred percent urbanized." Curiously, there is more biodiversity in Singapore than in all of the United States.

From the early days Singapore recognized the threat posed by cars. Hence both the ownership and the use of cars are severely taxed. To buy a car, one has to first buy a piece of paper — a Certificate of Entitlement (COE). A limited number of COEs are auctioned every month, to control car population growth. Today an average COE costs U.S.$30,000. Including taxes, a Mercedes-Benz now costs more than U.S.$150,000. In 1998 an Electronic Road Pricing Scheme (ERPS) was launched to control car usage and manage traffic congestion. This penalizing of car transport is balanced by the provision of efficient subway and bus services, which, surprisingly, are not subsidized. Bus companies make money because the word "subsidy" is virtually taboo in Singapore.

This careful attention to the people's physical and material needs is matched by equal care and concern for their social and spiritual needs. In this, however, Singapore has consciously moved away from the welfare-state prescriptions of OECD societies. There are no homeless, destitute, or starving people in Singapore. Poverty has been eradicated, not through an entitlements program (there are virtually none), but through a unique partnership between government, corporate citizens, self-help groups, and voluntary initiatives. The state acts as the catalyst — matching financial support, sponsoring preventive and social care, and ensuring that people's basic needs are met. Remarkably, the poorest 5 percent of households have about the same levels of ownership of homes, television sets, refrigerators, telephones, washing machines, and video recorders as the national average. Perhaps this, combined with the tough law-and-order regime, explains why Singapore has one of the lowest crime rates in the world — 1,005 crimes per annum per 100,000 population.

Singaporean society emphasizes the importance of the family. Government policies are skewed in favor of encouraging extended families to live in the same neighborhood. These policies also encourage families to care for their own elderly. The traditional Asian emphasis on clan and kinship provides a valuable social glue, even as society modernizes and develops.

An equally strong emphasis is placed on multiracial harmony, given the experience with race riots before independence. The government publishes notices in the four official languages (Mandarin, Malay, Tamil, and English). Every Singaporean child has to be bilingual, and there is no ethnic discrimination in school or in the civil service. To avoid the evolution of racial ghettos in public housing, all estates are required to have a certain percentage of minority population. Citizen and community groups are encouraged to be multiracial. Every constituency is also provided with a community center, open to all citizens. A dense network of citizen consultative groups enables citizens to participate in managing the affairs of their community.

Singapore is not a perfect society. Nor is it a paradise. Affluence has created bad social habits: excessive consumption and waste generation. According to the United Nations Environment Programme (UNEP), Singaporeans generated 1.1 kilograms of domestic waste per person per day, compared to Germany's 0.9 kilograms. Littering lingers as a bad habit. Singapore is also not spared from the social problems of modern cities — drug abuse, juvenile delinquency, vandalism, and teenage crime — even though the deterrents are severe.

The struggle for survival and social improvement will be an eternal one for Singapore. But the successes that the country has had carry a message of hope. If the rest of the world could agree to accept the living conditions of Singaporeans, then the six billion people of our planet might need only an area the size of South Africa to live in. Somehow this possibility does suggest that the problems of our planet may be manageable and the divide may yet be bridged.

THE TEN COMMANDMENTS
FOR DEVELOPING COUNTRIES
IN THE NINETIES

In 1990 I was invited to attend the regular annual UNDP conference in Antalya, Turkey, a truly beautiful corner of the world. I knew little about developmental theory, but I did know that the conventional developmental theory that had been passed on to Third World societies had truly not worked well. Indeed, the real tragedy of many developing countries was that after the immediate euphoria of independence of colonial rule, they found the business of self-government to be difficult. A few progressed, but many more slid backward. It seemed to me unfair and unjust that Third World minds continued to be dished out conventional wisdom that had not worked in practice. Hence I decided to offer some unconventional thoughts on development. To my surprise, these thoughts traveled well. They were published in many magazines and also in Change: Threat or Opportunity for Human Progress, *edited by Uner Kirdar (vol. II, United Nations, New York, 1992).*

1. Thou shalt blame only thyself for thy failures in development. Blaming imperialism, colonialism, and neo-imperialism is a convenient excuse to avoid self-examination.

2. Thou shalt acknowledge that corruption is the single most important cause of failures in development. Developed countries are not free from corruption, but with their affluence they can afford to indulge in savings and loan scandals.

3. Thou shalt not subsidize any product, nor punish the farmer in order to favor the city dweller. High prices are the only effective signal to increase production. If there are food riots, thou shalt resign from office.

4. Thou shalt abandon state control for free markets. Thou shalt have faith in thine own population. An alive and productive population naturally causes development.

5. Thou shalt borrow no more. Thou shalt get foreign investment that pays for itself. Thou shalt build only the infrastructure that is needed and create no white elephants or railways that end in deserts. Thou shalt accept no aid that is intended only to subsidize ailing industries in developed countries.

6. Thou shalt not reinvent the wheel. Millions of people have gone through the path of development. Take the well-traveled roads. Be not prisoners of dead ideologies.

7. Thou shalt scrub the ideas of Karl Marx out of thy mind and replace them with the ideas of Adam Smith. The Germans have made their choice. Thou shalt follow suit.

8. Thou shalt be humble when developing and not lecture the developed world on their sins. They listened politely in the 1960s and 1970s. They no longer will in the 1990s.

9. Thou shalt abandon all North-South forums, which only encourage hypocritical speeches and token gestures. Thou shalt remember that the countries that have received the greatest amount of aid per capita have failed most spectacularly in development. Thou shalt throw out all theories of development.

10. Thou shalt not abandon hope. People are the same the world over. What Europe achieved yesterday, the developing world will achieve tomorrow. It can be done.

NOTES

Preface

1. "Tomayto, Tomahto, Potayto . . . ," *New York Times*, "The Week in Review," 13 August 2000, p. 2.

Introduction

1. Fareed Zakaria, "The Rise of Illiberal Democracy," *Foreign Affairs*, November/December 1997.

2. James Fallows was my fellow panelist at this seminar, and judging from his response it would be fair to say that he was shocked by this essay.

3. Max Weber, *Politics as a Vocation* (Philadelphia: Fortress Press, 1965), p. 49

4. Reinhold Niebuhr, *The Irony of American History* (New York: Charles Scribner's Sons, 1952), chapter 4.

Can Asians Think?

1. Will Durant, *The Age of Faith* (New York: Simon & Schuster, 1950), p. 450.

2. Joseph Stiglitz, *Asian Wall Street Journal*, 2 February 1998.

3. Zbigniew Brzezinski, *Out of Control* (New York: Charles Scribner's Sons, 1993), p. 3.

4. Ibid., pp. 4–5.

An Asian Perspective on Human Rights and Freedom of the Press

1. Kishore Mahbubani, "The West and the Rest," The *National Interest* no. 28, summer 1992, p. 10.

2. Melvin Richter, "Despotism," in *Dictionary of the History of Ideas*, edited by Philip P. Wiener (New York: Charles Scribner's Sons, 1973), p. 1.

3. Edward W. Said, *Covering Islam: How the Media and the Experts Determine How We See the Rest of the World* (New York: Pantheon Books, 1981), p. xvii.

4. Nancy Caldwell Sorel, "First Encounters: Josef Stalin and Winston Churchill," The *Atlantic Monthly*, November 1991, p. 141.

5. Max Weber, *Politics as a Vocation* (Philadelphia: Fortress Press, 1965), p. 49.

6. Ibid., p. 47.

Pol Pot: The Paradox of Moral Correctness

1. Stan Sesser, "Report from Cambodia," *New Yorker*, 18 May 1992, p. 48.
2. Elizabeth Becker, "Up from Hell," *The New Republic*, 7 February 1992, p. 33.
3. Ibid., p. 36.
4. Weber, *Politics as a Vocation*, p. 53.

The Rest of the West?

1. William H. McNeill, *The Rise of the West: A History of the Human Community* (University of Chicago Press, 1963), 1991.
2. J. M. Roberts, *The Triumph of the West* (Little Brown & Co., 1985).
3. "The World: The U.S. and Africa: Extending a Trembling, Hesitant Hand," *New York Times*, "The Week in Review," 7 May 2000, p. 3.
4. *Financial Times Weekend*, 13/14 May, 2000, p. xxvii.
5. *New York Times*, 7 May 2000, section 3, p. 4.
6. Speech by UN Secretary-General Kofi Annan to Millennium Forum on 22 May 2000 in New York.
7. Claude Smadja, "The End of Complacency," *Foreign Policy*, winter 1998–99, p. 67.
8. Peter G. Peterson, *Gray Dawn* (Random House, 1999), pp. 52–55.
9. "Europe's Immigrants," *The Economist*, 6–12 May 2000, p. 25.
10. William H. McNeill, pp. 730-31.
11. J. M. Roberts, p. 14.
12. Ibid., p. 278.
13. Ibid., p. 730.
14. Ibid., p. 289.
15. Simon Worral, "London on a Roll," *National Geographic*, June 2000, p. 10.

"The Pacific Impulse"

1. Kenneth S. Courtis, "The Centre of the World Economy Shifts to the Asia-Pacific: Challenges and Opportunities for Canada," an address to the Pacific Basin Economic Council of Canada, Toronto, 18 April 1994.
2. Richard K. Betts, "Wealth, Power and Instability," *International Security*, vol. 18, no. 3, winter 1993–94, p. 64.
3. Aaron L. Friedberg, "Ripe for Rivalry," *International Security*, vol. 18, no. 3, winter 1993–94, p. 7.
4. Barry Buzan and Gerald Segal, "Rethinking East Asian Security," *Survival*, vol. 36, no. 2, summer 1994, p. 7.
5. William Rees-Mogg, "Money Moves East, as Welfare goes West," *The Straits Times* (Singapore), 9 July 1994, p. 35.
6. Stephanie Gazelline, "World Competitiveness Today: New Rules for a New Era," *European Business Report*, spring 1994, p. 22.

7.   Rees-Mogg, op. cit.

8.   Richard J. Samuels, *Rich Nation, Strong Army: National Security and the Technological Transformation of Japan* (Cornell University Press, 1994).

9.   Buzan and Segal, op. cit.

10.   Daniel Pipes, "Why the Stakes Are So High in Algeria," *International Herald Tribune*, 13 August 1994.

11.   "Islam and the West," The *Economist*, 6–12 August 1994.

12.   Kishore Mahbubani, "The West and the Rest," *The National Interest*, no. 28, summer 1992, pp. 5–6.

13.   William Pfaff, "Africa Needs Europe to Get Involved Again in a Different Spirit," *International Herald Tribune*, 15 August 1994, p. 4.

14.   Betts, op. cit.

UN: Sunrise or Sunset Organization in the Twenty-first Century?

1.   Kishore Mahbubani, the permanent representative of Singapore to the United Nations in New York, contributed this essay in his personal capacity as the author of "Can Asians Think?" not in his official capacity as a UN representative.

2.   It is vital to note that when the U.S. scale of assessment was last reduced to 25 percent for the regular budget in 1972, the U.S. delegate said categorically that this move to 25 percent would be "the final step." See twenty-seventh UN General Assembly Document A/8952 of 12 December 1972.

3.   See article entitled "U.S. Doesn't Bear Excessive Share Of U.N. Costs" by Kishore Mahbubani, *Wall Street Journal*, 30 October 1986.

4.   Just look, for example, at the index for "Twentieth Century: The History of the World 1901 to 2000" by J. M. Roberts.

5.   "The UN and American Politics," by Gene M. Lyons, Global Governance 5 (1999), p. 501.

6.   Ibid., p. 500.

7.   Report of the secretary-general on the Millennium Assembly entitled "We the peoples: the role of the United Nations in the twenty-first century," 27 March 2000.

INDEX

ABM Treaty, 177
academic performance
  East Asian civilization, 24
  IC factor, 109
Africa
  and Europe, 144, 146–147
  middle classes, lack of, 50
  population, 109
African Americans, reported emancipation
  of, 64–65
The Age of Faith (Durant), 20–21
agricultural subsidies
  abandonment of, 76, 146
  in Third World, 190
AIDS, UN Security Council debate on, 180
Algeria
  democracy, experience with, 52
  fundamentalist revolution in, 145
  vs. Peru's reversal of democratization,
    52–53
  population of, 46
  sanctions, lack of, 71
altruism, as mask, 179–180
America. *See* United States
American Bureau of the Budget, 141
Angkor Wat, 34, 35
Annan, Kofi, 106, 174, 178, 185
Arabs. *See* Islamic societies
ASEAN Regional Forum (ARF), 144, 156
Asia-Pacific
  See also Asian societies; East Asia;
    Southeast Asia
  change in, 159–160
  corporate culture on regional security,
    152
  culturally diverse pairs, 156
  diversity, familiarity with, 145
  Four Tigers, emergence of, 23
  freer trade, timetable for, 157
  networks, 155

  peace in, 159–160
  status quo, preservation of, 159–160
  uniqueness, 156
  vision of community, 150–152
Asia-Pacific Economic Cooperation
  Conference (APEC), 144, 155–156, 157,
    162
"Asian and American Perspectives
  on Capitalism and Democracy"
  seminar, 58
Asian financial crisis, 107–108, 137,
  171–172
Asian identity, 113–114
Asian population, 19
Asian renaissance, 27, 112
Asian societies
  See also China; East Asia; Japan
  challenges, 28
    political stability, 30
    social, 31
  confidence, renewed, 26
  corruption, 37–38
  culture
    divisions within Asia, 135
    strength, 112
  decline of, 21
  difficult relations, dealing with, 154
  economic
    challenges, 28
    development, commitment to,
      77–78
  emulation of West, 25
  "face," importance of, 154
  feudal mind-set, 37
  heritage, rediscovery of, 26
  hierarchy, acceptance of, 154–155
  human rights policies as Western
    concepts, 74
  integration with global economy, 29
  learning process, 35

legacy, richness of, 26
mental colonization, 22–23
meritocracy, 113
middle classes, lack of, 50
nepotism, 113
noninterference in internal affairs,
     153–154
optimism, 27
political stability, challenges of, 30
racial divisions within Asia, 135
reconnection with past, 112
rule of law, 38, 113
social challenges, 31
spiritual strength, 112
symbolic gestures, importance of, 155
and war, 31
Asian values
    debate, 14–15, 16, 32
    development of, 31
    financial crisis and, 31–32
    integration with modern world, 33
    reassertion of, 32–33
    true test of, 32
Asian Wall Street Journal, 24
Association of Southeast Asian Nations
    (ASEAN), 131, 144, 154, 155
Atlantic impulse
    Cold War, end of, 148
    global interests, damage to, 147
    institutions, strong, 155
    military institutions, 148
    political institutions, 148
    Uruguay Round, GATT, 147–148
Atlantic Monthly, 13
Aung San Suu Kyi, 76
authoritarian governments, and
    development, 51
autonomy, loss of, 29
Ayodhya incident, 66

Baker, James, 118, 148
Balladur, Edouard, 96, 145
Barre, Mohd. Siad, 71
Becker, Elizabeth, 87
Betts, Richard, 139
BIS, 104
Bosnia, European passivity and, 144
Britain, economic development, 23
Brzezinski, Zbigniew, 27–28
Buzan, Barry, 139–140, 142–143

Cambodia, 43
    the Chams, 83
    communism

Pol Pot, fundamental mistake of, 88
        rejection of, 90
    dispassionate analysis, need for, 87–88
    extinction, fear of, 83
    genocide in, 53, 67
    Khmer Rouge
        attacks against delegates, 86–87
        intelligent tactics against, 89–90
        Pol Pot, cooperation with, 83
        Western refusal to work with
            Pol Pot, 81
    mitigating circumstances, 70
    moral responsibility for genocide, 53
    peace conference, failure of, 72, 82
    Pol Pot, cooperation with, 83
    recovery, 81
    United Nations
        peace agreement, 85–87, 89, 90
        supervised elections, 85–86
    and Vietnam
        exploitation of Western
            concerns, 84
        peace conference, role in failure
            of, 72, 82
        and Pol Pot's route to power, 82–83
        sole motive of invasion, 83
    and the West
        public opinion, role of, 82–85
        refusal to work with Pol Pot, 81
"Can Asians Think?" (Mahbubani),
    negative reactions to title, 18
capitalism, 36, 57
Carter, Jimmy, 64
challenges facing Asian societies, 28, 30,
    31
the Chams, 83
change
    in Asia-Pacific, 159–160
    democratic resistance to, 141
    demographic relationships, 108–109
    economic, 105–106
    and globalization, 106
    and interdependence, 107
    resistance to, 36, 141
*Change: Threat or Opportunity for Human
    Progress* (Kirdar), 190
China
    See also Asian societies; East Asia
    Confucian-Islamic connection,
        suggestion of, 95
    consumer market in, 149
    cosmopolitan era, potential return
        of, 161
    crisis, word for, 30, 160

East Asia
  alliances, effect of, 162
  economic success, impact of, 48
economic
  development, pace of, 23
  performance, 23
  synergies, 126
"flexible power" *(quan bian)*, 124
former technological prowess, 21–22
free press in, 66
good governance, 32
IC factor, 109
and Japan
  apology from, need for, 129, 134
  cross-cultural understanding,
    133–134
  disdain of, 126
  hierarchy, question of, 154–155
  misunderstanding, potential
    for, 127
  need for strong Japan, 160
  nuclear status of, 125, 160
  perception of, 125
  and U.S. alliance, 161–162
Korea, reunified, 124
military strength, 22
most-favored-nation status, 149
pragmatism, 32
sanctions against, 95
sixteenth century, 21–22
Taiwan. *See* Taiwan
Tang dynasty, 161
Tiananmen Square, 68, 95
United States
  cultural comfort, 160–161
  and Japan relationship, 161–162
  normalization of ties with, 121
  one-China policy, 162–163
and Vietnam, 126
Western behavior toward, 94–95
World Trade Organization, entry
  into, 163
in year 997, 20
Churchill, Winston, 68–69
Citicorp, 64
clannishness, 31
Clark, William Smith, 151
"The Clash of Civilizations?"
  (Huntington), 14, 40, 92, 93
Clinton, Bill, 157, 175
Cold War
  Cambodia, 43
  conflicts supported by, 43
  immoral policies during, 71

post–Cold War era. *See* post–Cold
  War era
Third World, importance of, 42
colonization, 22
  Asian societies, 22–23
  blame on, 190
  emancipation from mental, 75
  end of, 44
  Goa, 22
  mental, 22–23, 75
  non–permanence of, 47
  by Portugal, 22
  scholarship, cooperation with, 67–68
common Asian home, sense of, 134, 135
communism
  effect of collapse of, 49
  and Pol Pot regime, 88
  prediction of behavior, 89
  Southeast Asia, 153
competitive advantages, 35
Comprehensive Test Ban Treaty, 177
confidence, renewed, 26
Confucian civilizations. *See* China
Confucian-Islamic connection,
  suggestion of, 95
consumer markets, 149
cooperation with existing governments, 77
corruption
  Asian societies, 37–38
  and failure of development, 190
  and Western media, 62–63
Courtis, Kenneth, 151
Covering Islam (Said), 66–67
Cramer, Jean Antoine, 64
crime, 25, 75, 97, 189
"crisis" Chinese understanding of word,
  30, 160
de Cuellar, Javier Perez, 169
culture
  Asian renaissance, 27, 112
  cultural confidence
    educational excellence as
      prerequisite, 24
    IC factor, 109
  growing interest in, 27
  Western dominance in, 25

D'Amato Act, 163
"The Dangers of Decadence: What
  the Rest Can Teach the West"
  (Mahbubani), publication of, 14
Davos World Economic Forum, 17, 185,
  186
Demming, Arthur, 151

democracy
  change, resistance to, 141
  and corruption, 37–38
  EC Common Agricultural Policy, 56–57
  before economic development, 49–50
  exportation of, 13
  human rights, restrictions on, 52
  immediate, complications of, 52
  as ingredient for success, 36
  institutional defects of, 55–57
  middle class, vested interest of, 50
  and national interests, 53
  new elites, 36
  promotion of, 49
  prudence in promotion of, 53
  radical reform, requirement of, 50
  short-term *vs.* long-term policies, 55
  transition to, problems of
    successful, 49
  universal applicability, challenges to,
    59–60
  U.S. budget deficit, as example of
    institutional defect, 55–56
  values of, 49
demographic relationships, changing,
  108–109
Deng Xiaoping, 37, 76, 95
despotism, 60
Dictionary of the History of Ideas, 60
domination. *See* Western domination
double standards, 70, 71, 94, 144
drug addiction, 25
Dulles, John Foster, 121
Durant, Will, 20–21, 35

East Asia
  See also Asia-Pacific
  Academic performance, 24
  alliances within, effect of, 162
  confidence, explosion of, 140–141
  consumer market in, 149
  economic development, pace of,
    23, 139
  economic performance in past
    decades, 23
  Europe, comparisons with, 139
  "face," importance of, 154
  fusion of East and West, 150, 152
  gross domestic product, rise in, 141
  Japan's economic success, impact
    of, 48
  Pacific community, vision of, 150–152
  peace in, 152
  psychological revolution, 140

  security, linkage to European, 152
  United States, continued engagement
    of, 162
East Asian Economic Caucus, 156, 162
East Timor, 154, 174
Ebola virus, 171
economic challenges, 28
  autonomy, loss of, 29
  globalization as factor, 29
  international financial markets,
    accountability to, 29
  Thai baht, devaluation of, 28–29
economic change, 105–106
economic development
  agricultural subsidies, abandonment
    of, 76
  authoritarian governments,
    commitment of, 73–74
  commitment to, 77–78
  costs of promotion of, 55, 76–77
  before democracy, 49–50
  expectation of, impact of fostering, 48
  GATT as trigger of, 56–57
  and human rights, 76–77
  liberation of Third World, 76
  pace of, among East Asian societies,
    23–24
economic problems, in Western
  societies, 25
Economist, 87, 109, 145
educational excellence. *See* academic performance
Egypt, growing population of, 45
emulation of West, 25
the environment, 108, 171, 188
ethical standards, decline in, 25
Ethiopia, 43
Europe
  advances in, 22
  and Africa, 45, 144, 146–147
  agricultural subsidies, abandonment
    of, 146
  "Atlantic impulse," 147–148
  and Bosnia, passivity toward, 144
  conflict surrounding, 143
  consumer market in, 149
  "Dark Ages," 20
  disposable income, drop in, 141
  disputes with United States, 114
  domination by, 21
  East Asia, comparisons with, 139
  free trade, barriers to, 145–146
  government spending, 141
  immigration

from Africa, 147
illegal, 146
need for, 109
internal unification, focus on, 143–144
Islam
exclusion of, 144–145
paranoia about, 94
job creation in, 141
moral leadership, 145
optimism, 27
population, changing ratios, 45, 146
regional institutions, existence of, 143
and Russia, 144
sixteenth century, 21
social idea, belief in superiority of, 145
social safety nets, 26
socioeconomic policies, 141
subsidies, 145–146
United States, disputes with, 114
war during growth period, 37
Europe Asia Forum, 158
European Community
Common Agricultural Policy, 56–57
Uruguay Round GATT talks, failure
of, 57
Evans, Gareth, 137

Fallows, James, 58
family, breakdown of, 25
Federalist, 50
feudal mind-set, 37
Financial Stability Forum, 104
financial vulnerability
and good governance, 32
and political systems, 32
Fire in the Lake, 67
Foreign Affairs, 17, 92, 137
Foreign Policy, 118
Four Tigers, emergence of, 23
France
Algeria, fundamentalist revolution
in, 145
population of, 46
free markets
as ingredient for success, 36
nonemulation of system, 47
as Third World goal, 191
free press. *See* Western media
freedom
individual, 97
of the press. *See* Western media
Friedberg, Aaron L., 139
From Third World to First (Lee), 185, 187
Fujimori, 52–53, 73

Fukuyama, Francis, 41
Fukuzawa, Yukichi, 25, 129, 151
fusion of civilizations, as hope of
future, 17

G-7 countries
economic power, 104
international community, no
legitimacy to represent, 174–175
United States, Atlantic impulse, 148
GATT
and economic development, 56–57
"level playing field," creation of, 57
Uruguay Round, 56, 57, 96, 147–148
General Motors, 64
genocidal rulers, cooperation with, 68–70,
83
Germany, World War II, lesson of, 37
global
communication networks, 44–45
society, creation of, 44–45
village, effects of, 44
globalization
change in twenty-first century, 106
and economic issues, 29
the environment, 108
globalized Asian mind, emergence
of, 30
and interdependence, 107, 170–172
irreversible force of, 106–107
positive effects of, 107
talent, emergence of new, 36–37
traffic analogy, 171
United Nations, impact on, 170–172
virtues *vs.* vices of, 106
"Go East, Young Man" (Mahbubani), publication of, 14
Goa, colonization of, 22
good governance/government
China, 32
and financial vulnerability, 32
and free press, 65
and migration, 51
operational definition, 51
in Third World, 51
Gorbachev, Mikhail, 124, 145
Greenpeace, 180

Hammarskjold, Dag, 168
Hare, R. M., 69
Harries, Owen, 14
Head, Ivan, 46
Helms, Jesse, 178
Helms-Biden Act, 168

Helms-Burton Act, 163
Holbrooke, Richard, 168, 178
honesty, 37–38
Hong Kong
    emergence as economic tiger, 23
    financial crisis, impact of, 32
human annihilation, 28
human rights policies
    and abandonment of Third World
        allies, 71
    absurd aspect of, 59
    Asian awareness, lack of, 74
    benefits of, 54
    consequences
        immoral, 71–73
        sanctions, moral responsibility
            for, 53
    cynicism about, 52
    and economic development, 76–77
    immoral consequences of, 71–73
    inconsistencies, effect of, 53–54
    minimal codes of civilized conduct,
        78
    moral responsibility for consequences
        of sanctions, 53
    mutual respect, 74–76
    and national interests, 53
    in practice, 51
    promotion of, 48–49
    restriction under democratic rule, 52
    sacrifice of, willing, 70–71
    symbolic victories, 76
    from Third World perspective, 54
    universal applicability, challenges to,
        59–60
humanitarian intervention, 81
Hun Sen, 83, 84, 86, 89
Huntington, Samuel P., 14, 40, 92,
    93, 122
Hurgronje, C. Snouck, 67
Hussein, Saddam, 121

"I love you" computer virus, 107
IBM, 64
IC factor, 109
immigration. *See* migration and
    immigration
imperfect government, as better moral
    choice, 73
India
    Ayodhya incident, 66
    consumers in, 149
    economic growth in, 107
    free press in, 65–66

IC factor, 109
    post–Cold War era, 44
    returning students, impact of, 36
individual freedoms, 97
Indonesia
    China's economic success, impact
        of, 48
    earlier bleak prospects, 153
    economic
        challenges, 28–29
        development, pace of, 23
        performance, 23
Industrial Revolution, 22, 31
infectious diseases, 108
influence, Western, 101
information
    flow, 105
    Western control of, 105
institutional defects of democracy, 55–57
integration
    and Asian values, 33
    with global economy, 29
intellectual division, 18
intellectual liberty, beginnings of, 22
interconnectedness, 57
interdependence
    Asian financial crisis, 171–172
    economic field and, 107
    and the environment, 108, 171
    and globalization, 107, 170–172
    growth of, 108
    Japan and United States, 122, 132
    and Western domination, 107–108
    Western transformation, 114
"International Conference on Cambodia"
    (Paris), 71–72, 82
"International Conference on Thinking"
    (7th), 18
international financial markets, account-
    ability to, 29
International Institute of Strategic Studies,
    17
international law, 44
International Monetary Fund, 104
    Thai baht, 29
Iran, restriction on human rights, 52
Ishihara, Shintaro, 121
"Islam and the West," 145
Islamic societies
    Confucian-Islamic connection,
        suggestion of, 95
    democratic elections in, 52
    East Asian economic success,
        potential impact of, 48

Europe, exclusion from, 144–145
media coverage of, 66–67
preservation of fruits of Greek and
Roman civilizations, 27
Western paranoia about, 94
in year 997, 20
Italy, declining population, 45

Japan
See also Asian societies; East Asia
and China
apology to, need for, 129, 134
cross-cultural understanding,
133–134
disdain for, 126
hierarchy, question of, 154–155
misunderstanding, potential for, 127
need for strong Japan, 160
nuclearization of Japan and, 125
refugees from, 126
Taiwan, relationship with, 126
and U.S. alliance, 161–162
common Asian home, sense of, 134, 135
cultural limitations, 130
defeat of Russia, psychological
impact of, 47
destiny and the West, 129
development equal to Western
civilization, 23
East Asia
alliances, effect of, 162
political influence in, 131
economic
development, 23
environment, adaptation to, 32
power, 119
success, 23
exclusivity of Japanese society, 130
fusion of East and West in, 150
global citizenship, 135–136
government intervention in, 56
human rights and, 74, 129
international conflicts, management
of, 135–136
international security, 121
kenbei, 121
Korea
cross-cultural understanding,
133–134
nuclear weapons, 124–125
reunified, 123–124
and Korea
apology to, need for, 129, 134
Korean War, 129–130

leadership, weak, 130
learning from West, 25
in level playing field, 151
Meiji Restoration, 23
military
conflict, public aversion to, 121
power, 128
nuclear status, 124–125, 128, 131–132,
160
Osaka summit, 157
political limitations, 130
post–Cold War era
gains, 119
identity and role in, 118, 119
strategy, change in, 120
United States, relationship with, 120
quality-control methods, 151
"Rich Nation, Strong Army"
(fukoku kyohei), 142
and Russia
cross-cultural understanding,
133–134
psychological impact of defeat
of, 47
relationship with, 123
security concerns, 123–127, 128
Singapore, conquest of, 41–42
socioeconomic reforms post–World
War II, 50
and Taiwan, 126
Third World, impact on, 47–48
United States
auto industry, 56
and China, relationship, 161–162
cultural comfort, 160–161
defense relationship, 128
economic tensions with, 133
equal partnership, demand for, 128
geographic interests, differences
in, 129, 134
interdependence, 122, 132
mutual condescension, 122
Persian Gulf War, 121–122
post–Cold War relationship with,
120, 132
pre–Cold War relationship with, 121
public opinion in, 132
racial differences, 127
restructure of relationship,
127–128, 132
submission to demands of, 121
threat to, public view of, 122
and Vietnam, 126
investment embargo on, 135

World War II
    lesson of, 37
    as painful topic, 129–130
    war crimes, issue of, 129–130
The Japan That Can Say No (Ishihara), 121
Jay, John, 50
Jews, collective suffering of, 19–20
Johnson, Lyndon, 64
journalists. *See* Western media

Kahn, Joseph, 106
Kaplan, Robert, 13, 106
Karadzic, Radovan, 70
Kennedy, John F., 63–64
Khieu Samphan, 86
Khmer Rouge. *See* Cambodia
Kim Il Sung, 124, 149
Kim Jong Il, 149
King, Rodney, 65
Kirdar, Uner, 190
Kohl, Helmut, 123, 145
Korea
    and Japan
        apology, need for, 129, 134
        cross-cultural understanding,
            133–134
        distrust of, 124
    Korean War, 120, 129–130
    North. *See* North Korea
    reunified
        Russian interest in, 124
        threat to Japan, 123–124
    South. *See* South Korea
Kuriyama, Takakazu, 122

language, growing interest in, 27
Law of Sea Conference, 179
learning process, 35
Lee Kuan Yew, 185, 187, 188
level playing field
    futile exercise of, 151
    GATT, 57
    requirement of, 61
liberalism. *See* Western liberalism
Lon Nol, 82
London, city of, 114–115
Luck, Ed, 176, 177
Lyons, Gene, 170

Macau, colonization of, 22
Malacca, colonization of, 22
Malaysia
    economic challenges, 28–29
    economic performance, 23

Mao Zedong, 76, 95
Marx, Karl, 105, 191
Mbabazi, Amama, 104
McNeill, William H., 100, 109–110,
    111, 114
Meiji Restoration, 23
mental colonization, 22–23
meritocracy, 36–37, 113
Mexico, population of, 46
middle classes, lack of, 50
migration and immigration
    from Africa, 147
    aversion through belief in economic
        development, 48
    better life, drive for, 45
    European need for, 109
    and good government, 51
    mass, 42
    prevention of mass, 56–57
    Third World, 42
Mill, John Stuart, 50
minimal codes of civilized conduct, 78
Mobutu, 71
Moi, Daniel Arap, 71
moral
    correctness. *See* Cambodia
    cowardice, 73
    issues
        black-and-white solutions, belief
            in, 17
        immoral results from moral
            correctness, 72–73
        imperfect government, as better
            moral choice, 73
        moral principles, calculated
            application of, 54
    rules, 69
    superiority, assumption of, 61
Morocco, population of, 46
multilateral economic agencies, 104
multinational corporations, and Asian
    talent, 37
musical brilliance, 25
mutual respect, 74–76
Mutual Security Treaty, 120, 128
Myanmar, 70, 78, 144

Naipaul, V. S., 16, 111
nation-state, 44, 103
National Geographic, 114–115
National Interest, 14, 18, 40
national sovereignty, 44
NATO, 103
Nehru, Jawaharlal, 25, 47

nepotism, 31, 113
Niebuhr, Reinhold, 15
Nimmanhaeminda, Tarrin, 30
Nixon, Richard, 64, 68, 121
nominal equality, 104
norms, global, 173
North Korea
    independence of, 124
    nuclear weapons, 124–125
North-South forums, abandonmenof, 191

"objective reporting," falsehood of, 66–68
optimism, 27
Organization for Economic Cooperation
    and Development (OECD), 104, 148
Ottoman Empire, 21
Out of Control (Brzezinski), 27–28

Pacific Basin Economic Council of
    Canada, 151
Pacific community, vision of. *See* Asia-
    Pacific
"The Pacific Impulse" (Mahbubani), publi-
    cation of, 17
Pakistan, post–Cold War era, 44
Paris Peace Conference. *See* "International
    Conference on Cambodia" (Paris)
parliamentary institutions, 44
Patten, Chris, 75
peace
    in Cambodia, 72, 82, 85–87, 89, 90
    in East Asia, 152
    international society and, 142–143
    in Southeast Asia, 153
    as status quo in Asia-Pacific, 159–160
    successful societies, 37
Perry, Matthew, 121
Persian Gulf War, 121–122
"Perspectives on Political Development
    and the Nature of the Democratic
    Process: Human Rights and Freedom
    of the Press" (Mahbubani), 14
Peru, sanctions against, 52–53, 73
Pfaff, William, 146
the Philippines
    free press in, 65
    socioeconomic reforms, failure of,
        50–51
Picco, Gianni, 169
Pol Pot, 69, 70, 71–72, 83
    see also Cambodia
"Pol Pot: The Paradox of Moral
    Correctness" (Mahbubani)
    publication of, 14

as response, 17
political stability, challenges of, 30
political systems and financial vulnerabil-
    ity, 32
Politics as a Vocation (Weber), 72, 91
population
    Africa, 109
    Asians as percentage of, 19
    Bangladesh, 186
    changing ratios, 45–46, 108–109, 146
    extreme imbalances, impact of, 46–47
    global average, 186
    Singapore, 186
    Southeast Asia, 153
    and Western domination, decline in,
        108–109
"population explosion," cliché of, 46
Portugal, colonization by, 22
post–Cold War era
    abandonment of Third World, 43
    India, 44
    instability in Third World, 44
    Japan. *See* Japan
    new threats, aggravation of, 56
    Pakistan, 44
    population imbalances, 46–47
    problems, wrongful identification
        and definition, 41
    reorientation of Western strategy, 57
power
    architecture of power relationships,
        103, 104–105
    continuation of old forms of, 104
    economic, 103–104
    exercise of, changes in means of, 103
    imbalance, 105
    military, 103
    resources, deployment of, 104
    "soft," 104
    and United Nations, 168–170
power shifts
    See also Asia-Pacific; East Asia
    China, 94–96
    Islam, 94–96
pragmatism, 32, 54
prediction for twenty-first century, 111
Prowse, Michael, 106
psychological factors
    Japan's economic success, 47–48
    Russia's defeat by Japan, 47
public opinion. *See* Western public opinion

Rees-Mogg, William, 141
resources, deployment of, 104

Rest of the West, 101
The Rise of the West (McNeill), 100,
    109–110
Roberts, J. M., 100, 110–111, 112, 113, 114
Roosevelt, Franklin D., 121
rule of law, 38, 113
Russia
    and Europe, 144
    and Japan
        cross-cultural understanding,
            133–134
        relationship with, 123

sacred cows in Western discourse, 59, 60
Said, Edward W., 66–67
Samuels, Richard J., 142
Saudi Arabia, human rights in, 51
science, domination in, 105
Segal, Gerald, 139–140, 142–143
Serbia, 70
Shigeru, Yoshida, 121
Silicon Valley, 109, 114
Singapore
    affluence in, 189
    cars, ownership of, 188
    Central Providence Fund, 187
    crime in, 75, 189
    economic success, 186–187
    emergence as economic tiger, 23
    the environment, 188
    family, importance of, 189
    financial crisis, impact of, 32
    health system, 187
    Japanese conquest analogy, 41–42
    and media depiction, 186
    multiracial harmony, emphasis
        on, 189
    odds, beating the, 186–187
    population, 186
    poverty, 188
    socioeconomic policies, 187
    spiritual needs of people, 188–189
sixteenth century, 21
Smadja, Claude, 107
Smith, Adam, 191
Smith, Chris, 170
social
    challenges, 31
    choices, respect for, 75
    problems, Western societies, 25
    safety nets, 26
"soft" power, 104
Solarz, Stephen, 72

Somalia
    disintegration of, 44
    usefulness during Cold War, 73
Sorel, Nancy Caldwell, 68–69
South Korea
    authoritarian governments
        commitment of, 73–74
        and development, 51
    economic
        challenges, 28–29
        development, pace of, 23
        tiger, emergence as, 23
    financial crisis, impact of, 32
    globalization of modern economics,
        29–30
Southeast Asia
    communism, 153
    corporate culture for regional
        security, 153
    diversity, 153
    noninterference in internal affairs,
        erosion of principle of, 153–154
    peace in, 153
    population, 153
Soviet Union. *See* Cold War; Russia
Stalin, Joseph, 68–69
Stiglitz, Joseph, 24
subsidies, 145–146, 190
    See also agricultural subsidies
successful societies
    democracy in, 36
    free markets and, 36
    functional elites, 37
    honesty, 37–38
    meritocracy, 36–37
    peace, 37
    rule of law, 38
Suharto, 157
Sun Yat-sen, 25
Survival, 17, 137

Taiwan
    authoritarian governments
        commitment of, 73–74
        and development, 51
    economic tiger, emergence as, 23
    financial crisis, impact of, 32
    independence, flirtation with, 159
    and Japan, 126
    returning students, impact of, 36
Taiwan Relations Act, 163
Terrorism, 80
Thach, Nguyen Co, 71–72, 82

Thai baht, devaluation of, 28–29, 107
Thailand
  economic
    challenges, 28–29
    performance, 23
  financial crisis in, 29, 32
  globalization of modern economics,
    29–30
  Thai baht, devaluation of, 28–29, 107
Thatcher, Margaret, 69
Third World
  abandonment by West, 43, 71
  Cold War, importance during, 42
  debt, 191
  dollar output, increase in, 96
  economic development, costs of, 55
  exploitation of Cold War, 42
  free markets, 191
  and globalization, 107
  good government in, 51
  human rights, willing sacrifice of,
    70–71
  instability, 44
  and Japan's economic success, 47–48
  and non-governmental organizations,
    179
  North-South forums, abandonment
    of, 191
  performance of government, attention
    on, 51
  population surge, 46
  radical reform, requirement of, 50
  "social clause," Uruguay Round
    agreement, 147–148
  subsidies in, 190
  ten commandments for, 190–191
  United Nations and, 169–170
  and the West
    abandonment by, 43
    human rights policies, 54
    involvement, end of, 44
    media, power of, 62–63
    Western concepts in, 44
Tiananmen Square, 68, 95
trade, and ideas, 152
Triumph of the West (Roberts), 100, 110–111
Tsongas, Paul, 119
Turkenverehrung, in sixteenth century, 21

UN Development Program, 49
UN Millennium Summit, 107, 167
United Nations
  AIDS, Security Council debate on, 180

"anti-American" sentiment, media
    portrayal, 176
  burden-sharing process, 173–174
  Cambodia
    elections, 85–86
    peace agreement, 85–87
  Charter, 178
  as family of institutions, 172
  financial crisis, 168
  General Assembly, 173
  globalization
    common global interests, 178
    impact of, 170–172
  humanitarian work, 169
  intended weakness of, 167
  media portrayal, 176
  Millennium Report of secretary-
    general, 179
  norm-setting, 173
  participation by all nations, 175–176
  peacekeeping work of, 169, 174
  power, issue of, 168–170
  role of, 172–175
  Secretariat, 173
  secretary-general, 174
  Security Council, 172
  stabilizing role, 176
  strength of, 166
  survival, crippled, 167
  and Third World, 169–170
  traffic analogy, 171
  United States
    "anti-American" sentiment, media
      portrayal, 176
    as beneficiary of stabilizing
      role, 176
    damage done by, 169–170
    independence from, need for,
      176–177
    interest of, 166
    as last great hope, 170
    long-term interests of, 176
    paradoxes, dealing with, 178–180
    short-term *vs.* long-term interests
      of, 177–178
    Third World domination, reaction
      to, 169–170
  vulnerability of, 167
United States
  See also Western societies
  ABM Treaty, 177
  APEC, skepticism of, 162
  Atlantic *vs.* Pacific impulse, 148–150

auto industry
  and Japanese competition, 56
  Japanese methods, use of, 151
bad government, increasing, 64
benevolence, 161–162
budget deficit, 55–56, 64
China
  cultural comfort, 160–161
  normalization of ties with, 121
  one-China policy, 162–163
  World Trade Organization, entry
    into, 163
crime rate, 97
disputes with Europe, 114
divided decision-making process,
  162–163
East Asia
  alliances, effect of, 162
  continued engagement in, 162
economic development, 23
fiscal indiscipline, 64
fusion of East and West, 152
global interests, reconciliation
  with, 179
government intervention in, 56
Islam, paranoia about, 94
isolationism, resurgence of, 122
Japan
  cultural comfort, 160–161
  demands on, 121
  economic tensions with, 133
  as "free rider," 132
  geographic interests, differences
    in, 129, 134
  interdependence, 122, 132
  as "major threat," 122
  mutual condescension, 122
  post–Cold War relationship with,
    120, 132
  pre–Cold War relationship with, 121
journalists. *See* Western media
Mexico, free-trade agreement with, 146
open communication in, 162
Persian Gulf War, 121–122
private lobbies, 55–56
social institutions, disintegration of, 97
transpacific trade, 148–149
United Nations
  bashing, 170, 176
  beneficiary of stabilizing role, 176
  damage to, 169–170
  financial crisis of, 168
  globalization, impact of, 170–172
  independence of, 176–177

  and long-term interests, 177–178
  paradox of, 178–180
  strength of, 166
university, world's first, 20
Uruguay Round. *See* GATT

values
  Asian. *See* Asian values
  Western. *See* Western values
Van Ness, Peter, 58
"veil of ignorance," 38
Vietnam
  Cambodian invasion, sole motive in, 83
  conflict, in loss of "face," 154
  exploitation of Western concerns, 84
  and Japan, 126
  peace conference, role in failure of,
    72, 82
  and Pol Pot's route to power, 82–83
  Thach, Nguyen Co. *See* Thach,
    Nguyen Co
Vietnam War
  aftermath and Cambodia, 84–85
  media coverage of, 67

war
  Cold War. *See* Cold War
  democracy before economic
    development, 50
  during Europe's growth, 37
  and feudal mind-set, 37
  Korean War, 120
  Persian Gulf, 121–122
  in Vietnam. *See* Vietnam War
  in Western societies, 30–31
  World War II. *See* World War II
  zero aspect of, 31
Washington Quarterly, 14
weapons proliferation, 175
Weber, Max, 15, 72, 91
"The West and the Rest" (Mahbubani),
  publication of, 14
Western domination
  consequences of two centuries of, 101
  continual, 102–103
  demographic relationships, changing,
    108–109
  economic power, 103–104
  global influence, layers of, 101
  information and information
    technology, 105
  and interdependence, 107–108
  military power, 103
  multilateral economic agencies, 104

resources, deployment of, 104
science, 105
Western liberalism, 13–14
  seeing beyond, 26
Western media
  absolute power in Third World, 62–63
  African Americans, reported
    emancipation of, 64–65
  aggression of, and bad government,
    63–64
  Ayodhya incident, 66
  and China, 68
  corruption and, 62–63
  dishonesty of, 95
  distortion of perceptions, 59
  double standards of governments, 71
  hypocrisy of, 61–62
  increase in power, 58–59
  Islam, coverage of, 66–67
  marital infidelities, reports on, 61–62
  moral consequences of actions, 67
  moral cowardice, 73
  mutual respect, 74–76
  non-Americans, impact of actions
    on, 67
  "objective reporting," falsehood of,
    66–68
  as opium of American society, 63–64
  personal finances, politician's
    disclosure of, 62
  promotion of freedom of press, 60
  self-appointed guardian of free press,
    78–79
  Singapore, depiction of, 186
  Third World
    absolute power in, 62–63
    as allies, abandonment of, 71
  Tiananmen Square, 68, 95
  underdog, myth of journalist as, 62–63
  United Nations, "anti-Americanism"
    of, 176
  U.S. interests, effect of, 68
  Vietnam
    use of, 72
    war in, 67
  and the well-ordered society, 65–66
  Western assumptions, 94
Western public opinion
  Cambodia, role in, 82–85
  irrational consequences of, 95
  and Japan, 132
Western societies
  See also United States
  China, behavior toward, 94–95

crime, 25
culture, 25
drug addiction, 25
economic problems, 25, 97
ethical standards, decline in, 25
ethnic affinity, 31
family, breakdown of, 25
free press, self-appointed guardian
  of, 78–79
genocidal rulers, cooperation with,
  68–70
human rights, sacrifice of, 70–71
individual freedoms, 97
leadership, need for, 57
political development, atrophy of, 30
post–Cold War era. *See* post–Cold
  War era
preservation of fruits of Asian
  civilization, 26, 27
retreat, unwelcome, 93
social problems, 25
success of, 25
transformation, 114
war, zero aspect of, 30–31
Western values
  beliefs in, 33
  and blindness, 98
  democratic values, 49
  good *vs.* bad, 98
  pragmatic application of, 52
  structural weaknesses, 97
World Bank, 24, 104
world economy, center of, 17
world population. *See* population
World Trade Center, September 11, 2001,
  bombing of, 18, 92, 166
World Trade Organization, 104, 163
World War II
  Germany, lesson of, 37
  Japan
    lesson of, 37
    as painful topic, 129–130
    war crimes, issue of, 129–130

Yeltsin, Boris, 123
Yugoslavia, usefulness during Cold
  War, 73

Zakaria, Fareed, 13

A student of philosophy and history, Kishore Mahbubani has published extensively in leading journals and newspapers overseas (including *Foreign Affairs*, the *National Interest*, the *New York Times*, and the *Wall Street Journal*). He has also addressed many major international conferences, including Davos, Williamsburg, Ditchley, and the International Institute for Strategic Studies. These intellectual pursuits are a result of personal interest, not official duties.

By profession, Mr. Mahbubani is a civil servant and career diplomat who has been with the Singapore Foreign Service since 1971. He was Permanent Secretary of the Foreign Ministry from 1993 to 1998. His overseas postings have included Cambodia (where he served during the war, in 1973–74), Malaysia, the United States, and the United Nations. He has also traveled extensively around the world and attended high-level meetings in cities as varied as Seattle and Luanda, Havana and Bangkok, New Delhi and Luxembourg. He was the first dean of the Civil Service College in Singapore. He has served on the boards of several leading institutes and think tanks in Singapore, including the Institute of Southeast Asian Studies, the Institute of Policy Studies, the Lee Kuan Yew Exchange Fellowship, and the Institute of Defence and Strategic Studies.

Mr. Mahbubani was awarded the President's Scholarship in 1967, which enabled him to pursue undergraduate studies in philosophy at the University of Singapore (now the National University of Singapore). In 1976 he obtained a master's degree, also in philosophy, from Dalhousie University in Canada, which also awarded him an honorary doctorate in 1995. He was a fellow at the Center for International Affairs at Harvard University in 1991–92.

Mr. Mahbubani is currently serving as Singapore's ambassador to the United Nations, New York, and, concurrently, as Singapore's High Commissioner to Canada.